amazing LOOM KNITS

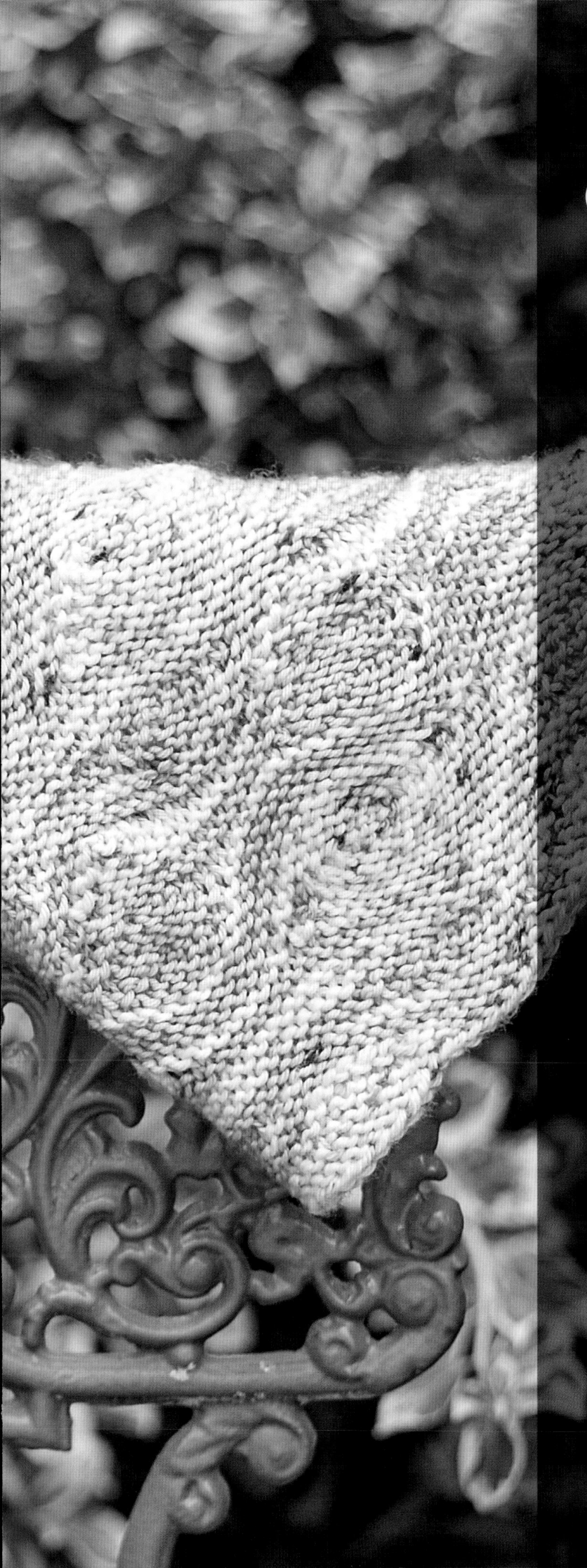

amazing LOOM KNITS

Cables, colorwork, lace, and other stitches

30 scarves, hats, mittens, bags, and shawls

Plus all the basics

Nicole F. Cox

STACKPOLE BOOKS

Guilford, Connecticut

Published by Stackpole Books
An imprint of The Rowman & Littlefield Publishing Group, Inc.
4501 Forbes Blvd., Ste. 200
Lanham, MD 20706
www.stackpolebooks.com

Distributed by NATIONAL BOOK NETWORK
800-462-6420

Illustrations, charts, and photography: Nicole F. Cox
Photography assistant: Raymond W. Cox Jr.
Styling and make-up: Nicole F. Cox, Danielle Kratky, and Amber Cox-Pretti
Models: Danielle Kratky, Amber Cox-Pretti, Danielle Decker, and Nicole F. Cox

British Library Cataloguing in Publication Information available

Library of Congress Cataloging-in-Publication Data available

Names: Cox, Nicole F., author.
Title: Amazing loom knits / Nicole F. Cox.
Description: First edition. | Guilford, Connecticut : Stackpole Books, [2019] | Includes bibliographical references and index.
Identifiers: LCCN 2018055408 | ISBN 9780811737975 (pbk. : alk. paper) | ISBN 9780811767965 (e-book)
Subjects: LCSH: Knitting—Patterns. | Handlooms.
Classification: LCC TT825 .C7274 2019 | DDC 746.43/2—dc23
LC record available at https://lccn.loc.gov/2018055408

™ The paper used in this publication meets the minimum requirements of American National Standard for Information Sciences—Permanence of Paper for Printed Library Materials, ANSI/NISO Z39.48-1992.

First Edition

Printed in the United States of America

This book is dedicated to my family . . . To my daughters, Amber and Danielle, whose strength, accomplishments, and love make the world a better place. Also, to my husband, who after 30 years is still fighting for more. You truly are "my one and only." And to Indus, my first grandchild, who spent many days cuddled on my lap while I wrote and edited this book. You are a joy, and I am thankful to have you as part of our family!

CONTENTS

INTRODUCTION

Hello and welcome to *Amazing Loom Knits*. For most loom knitters, including myself, accessories were our first projects. Maybe it was a simple hat or scarf. For me, it was making potholders for my mother when I was five years old; next, I progressed to skinny scarves. Like most new knitters, I was willing to undertake these new skills as seemed manageable in both time needed and project size. For this reason, I thought an accessories pattern book would be the perfect way to introduce loom knitters to fun new skills like brioche, Fair Isle, picking up stitches, lace, and so much more.

Included in this book are quick and easy patterns that use only simple stitches like knits, skip stitches, and purls. These make great last-minute projects to give as gifts, including a "no guilt" gift for yourself. We all need a breather sometimes, and simple projects that can be done in front of the television can provide a perfect way to relax at the end of the day.

There is something in this book for every loom knitter, beginner to advanced, with a variety of projects that will suit the casual country girl or the more sophisticated city girl. You'll find that a reasonable time investment will yield a wearable, unique piece that can't be found in stores. Most of these projects will also be forgiving in gauge and allow you to foray into more advanced skills without too much worry over fit.

There is full technical support for all the skills and techniques used in this book on my blog and YouTube channel. The addresses can be found in "Resources" at the back of this book. You'll find loom knitting articles, discussions, and videos to help you through any loom knitting challenge.

With this book, I'm hoping to finally dispel the myth that loom knitting is limited or just for simple items. Almost anything that can be made on needles or machine can also be done on a loom. It's an exciting time for loom knitters, as each year we have more talented designers and loom manufacturers giving us the tools we need for our craft. I hope you enjoy the patterns in this book as much as I enjoyed designing and writing them.

Happy looming!

—Nicole

READING MY PATTERNS

Understanding how to read a pattern is important for loom knitters who would like to further their skills. Often fiber artists feel defeated when they first glance at a pattern and see all those terms and abbreviations that they are not familiar with. Don't fear; with practice, you'll soon be sailing through these projects!

LEVEL

A skill level is given for all my patterns, from beginner to advanced. Use this as a guide only. I'm often asked whether a beginner can do a more advanced pattern. The answer is yes! All the skills needed to complete each pattern are included in this book. I encourage all loom knitters to get out of their comfort zone and try new things. Small projects, like the accessory patterns within this book, are a perfect way to advance your skills before moving onto larger projects like clothing.

FINISHED MEASUREMENTS

This is the final measurement of the finished piece—that is, after blocking (unless the pattern does not require blocking, as for most hats, mittens, and so forth). The patterns indicate when blocking is recommended.

GAUGE

Gauge is often ignored by loom knitters. It is easy to think that because our pegs are fixed that we are all knitting with the same tension and will get similar results. This is just not true, particularly if you change the yarn. I recommend knitting a 4-inch by 4-inch swatch and measuring to see whether you are achieving the proper gauge. Work the swatch with the given yarn and stitch. If your swatch is too small, you are working the stitches too tightly. If your swatch is too big, then you are working your stitches too loosely. Achieving gauge is important if you would like the finished piece to look like the original sample.

YARN

For each pattern, a specific yarn is recommended to achieve the pictured results. This will include fiber type, color, yardage, and number of skeins needed to complete your project. Changing the yarn is possible—feel free to be creative—but remember to use a similar yarn and check to see that you are achieving the proper gauge if you want similar results. As yarn weight, loft, and elasticity vary greatly in the same category, the only way to tell whether a chosen yarn will deliver equal results is to make a gauge swatch.

SUPPLIES AND LOOMS

Under "Supplies," you will find a list of supplies and notions needed to complete the pattern, including the loom needed. For convenience, I've written this book using a limited number of looms, all widely available in local craft stores. For each project, the loom is specified by the peg spacing (or the distance between the pegs) and the number of pegs. Large-gauge (3/4 in/2 cm) looms are appropriate for use with bulky yarns, while smaller-gauge (3/8 in/1 cm) looms are appropriate for light to medium-weight yarns. The pattern will also specify whether a round loom is required.

If you have a complete set of large-gauge looms (including the 48-peg, ⁵⁄₈ in/1.6 cm option) and an adjustable ³⁄₈ in/1 cm peg spacing loom, you will be able to work all the patterns in this book.

PATTERN NOTES

Any special notes for the pattern will be given in this section. Read these notes before beginning the pattern. Important construction notes (such as how the pattern is worked) will be here.

SPECIAL STITCHES/INSTRUCTIONS OR KEY

If the pattern has a special, repeatable stitch or technique, it will be listed in this section. For example, special stitches, like the seed stitch, will require a series of steps to achieve the desired result. Any special abbreviations will also be found here.

PATTERN

This is the main instruction area for the pattern. Read through the pattern before beginning, making sure that you understand all the abbreviations and instructions given. Research, within this book, any skills or abbreviations that you are not familiar with before starting the pattern.

FINISHING

All the final instructions for the pattern will be given here. This area will include seaming, blocking, and any other special instructions needed to finish your pattern.

CHARTS AND ILLUSTRATIONS

When necessary, you will find color/stitch charts and schematics to help you understand the written instructions and achieve the best results. All charts begin at the bottom right. You may work from the chart or the written instructions for all Fair Isle portions of a pattern. When a chart is included in a pattern that contains lace, use it for reference only. Loom knitters cannot slide stitches on a needle, as they are locked on individual pegs. To do lace, you must individually move each stitch to make room for yarn overs and other complex stitches. It is not possible to place all that information on a chart. Please use the chart as a tool to help you understand the direction of stitch movement and final placement of stitches only, and use the written instructions to complete the pattern.

BLOCKING

Blocking a knitted garment gives it a professional, finished look. You will need to block almost all lace garments to open the yarn overs and achieve straight edges. Occasionally blocking is necessary for your pattern to lie flat. Blocking is easy and can be achieved using the following instructions.

Soak your garment in cool or room temperature water using a touch of soap or fabric softener. Squeeze the piece gently to get the bulk of the water out; then roll it in a towel to remove as much water as possible. Using blocking mats and pins and/or wires, shape the finished piece into the desired measurements and shape. If the directions say to block lightly, stretch the garment lightly—do not overstretch. Be careful not to stretch areas like ribbing, or they'll lose their shape and won't spring back. Lace can usually be stretched aggressively; I like to open my yarn overs wide, making them highly noticeable. A simple rule of thumb: If your pins/wires or knitting begin to lift off the mat, then you are probably trying to stretch it too far. It's best to err on the side of caution before ruining a knitted piece. Let your garment dry completely before releasing it from the board.

ENJOY!

Take the time to admire your work. Loom knitting is a fiber art, and you should be proud of the time, preparation, and love that went into your finished piece.

THE PATTERNS

Winter Ushunka

A more refined version of the traditional trapper hat, this piece features a flat rounded crown, long earflaps, and a low back to keep your neck warm. Chunky yarn will make fast work of this lovely Russian-inspired hat, making it a great weekend project. If you're a fan of the traditional trapper, you can easily use browns and creams to get that look too!

Level

Confident Beginner

Finished Measurements

14 in/35.6 cm long x 22 in/55.9 cm around

Gauge

10 sts and 22 rows = 4 in/10.2 cm square in garter st

Yarn

Lion Brand Wool-Ease Thick & Quick, super bulky #6 (80% acrylic, 20% wool; 106 yd/97 m, 6 oz/170 g per skein)
1 skein #640 Cranberry (MC)
1 skein #153 Black (CC)

Lion Brand Fun Fur, bulky #5 (100% polyester; 64 yd/58 m, 1.75 oz/50 g per skein)
1 skein #153 Black (CC1)

Supplies

- ¾ in/2 cm peg spacing round loom with 40 pegs
- Knitting tool
- Crochet hook
- Measuring tape
- Stitch markers (optional)
- 3½ in/8.9 cm pom-pom maker or cardboard
- Yarn/tapestry needle

Pattern Notes

- Hat is worked from the bottom up in three separate sections that are eventually joined together.
- The top of the hat is decreased in four separate wedges and then seamed together.
- When asked to CO1, use the true cable cast-on method as described on page 110.
- For step-by-step instructions on working the single crochet edging and I-cord, see pages 127–28.

Pattern Stitch (seed stitch, multiples of 2)

Row 1: *K1, p1, rep from * to end of row.

Row 2: *P1, k1, rep from * to end of row (or purl the knits, knit the purls from the previous row).

Rep rows 1 and 2.

Pattern sequence will change depending on stitch count (odd or even number of sts).

Pattern

FRONT FLAP

Foundation row: Chain CO 8 pegs with 1 strand CC and 1 Strand CC1 held together; work as flat panel.

Row 1: *K1, p1, rep from * to last st, k1.

Row 2: CO1 stitch, *k1, p1, rep from * to end of row, CO1 stitch. (10 sts)

Row 3: K1, *k1, p1, rep from * to last stitch, k1.

Row 4: CO1 stitch, K1, *k1, p1, to last stitch, k1, CO1 stitch. (12 sts)

Row 5: *K1, p1, rep from * to last 2 sts, k2.

Rows 6–18: As row 5. (12 sts)

Cut working yarn but do not bind off.

EARFLAPS

Foundation row: Skip 1 peg behind front flap and chain CO 8 pegs with MC.

Row 1: *K1, p1, rep from * to last 2 sts, k2.

Row 2: CO1, *K1, p1, rep from * to last 2 sts, k2, CO1.

Row 3: Skip1, *k1, p1, rep from * to last st, k1.

Rows 4–25: As row 3. (10 sts)

Cut working yarn but do not bind off.

Rep above for second earflap.

BODY OF HAT

For bottom back and sides of hat, begin just behind front flap on second side. Work the earflaps and back of hat only for this portion. We will join the front in the next section. When beginning row 1 of this section, be sure to continue seed stitch pattern on the earflaps to avoid interruption in the fabric.

Row 1: Skip1, work in seed stitch to last stitch, k1, chain CO all empty pegs between earflaps, work in seed stitch to end of row.

Rows 2–10: Continue working in seed stitch.

Begin top of hat, paying attention to color changes.

Rnd 1 (MC): K3, *skip1 wyib, k3, rep from * to last st, skip1.

Rnd 2 (MC): *P3, skip1 wyib, rep from * to end of round.

Rnd 3 (CC): K1, *skip1 wyib, k3, rep from * to end of round, skip1, k2.

Rnd 4 (CC): P1, *skip1 wyib, p3, rep from * to end of round, skip1, p2.

Rnds 5–16: Rep rnds 1–4 (3 times).

Cut CC. Continue working with MC.

Rnd 17: Knit.

Rnd 18: Purl.

Rnds 19–34: Rep rnds 17 and 18 (8 times).

Begin decreasing.

Work in 4 sections of 10 pegs/stitches. You will have 4 separate wedges when finished.

Row 1: K10, turn.

Row 2: P10, turn.

Row 3: K2tog, knit to last 2 sts, ssk, turn. (8 sts)

Row 4: P8, turn.

Rows 5–10: Rep rows 3 and 4 (3 times). (6 sts, 4 sts, 2 sts)

Row 11: K2tog.

Bind off, leaving a long tail for seaming.

Rep 3 times, completing a total of 4 wedges.

Seam the top of hat closed using garter seam.

Weave in all ends on hat.

EAR POCKETS

Foundation row: Chain CO 4 sts.

Row 1: Skip1, k1, p1, k1.

Row 2: CO1, p1, k1, p1, k1, CO1. (6 sts)

Row 3: Skip1, p1, k1, p1, k1, p1.

Rows 4–14: As row 3 (11 times).

Chain one bind-off all pegs, leaving a long tail for seaming.

Single crochet around edge of pocket with CC and CC1 (1 strand of each held together).

Finishing

Single crochet all the way around bottom edge of hat beginning at the back and using 1 strand CC and 1 strand CC1 held together. When you get to front flap, fold it upward and single crochet along the bottom edge. This will help to keep it in place. Seam top of flap to main hat, being careful to hide stitches. Sew ear pockets onto upper center of earflap. Top of pocket should be even with bottom of front flap. Pick up 3 stitches from the bottom center of earflap and make a 9 in/22.9 cm 3-stitch I-cord (see page 127). Rep for second earflap. Make and attach a 2½ in/6.4 cm pom-pom to the bottom of each I-cord. Make and attach a 3½ in/8.9 cm pom-pom to the top of the hat.

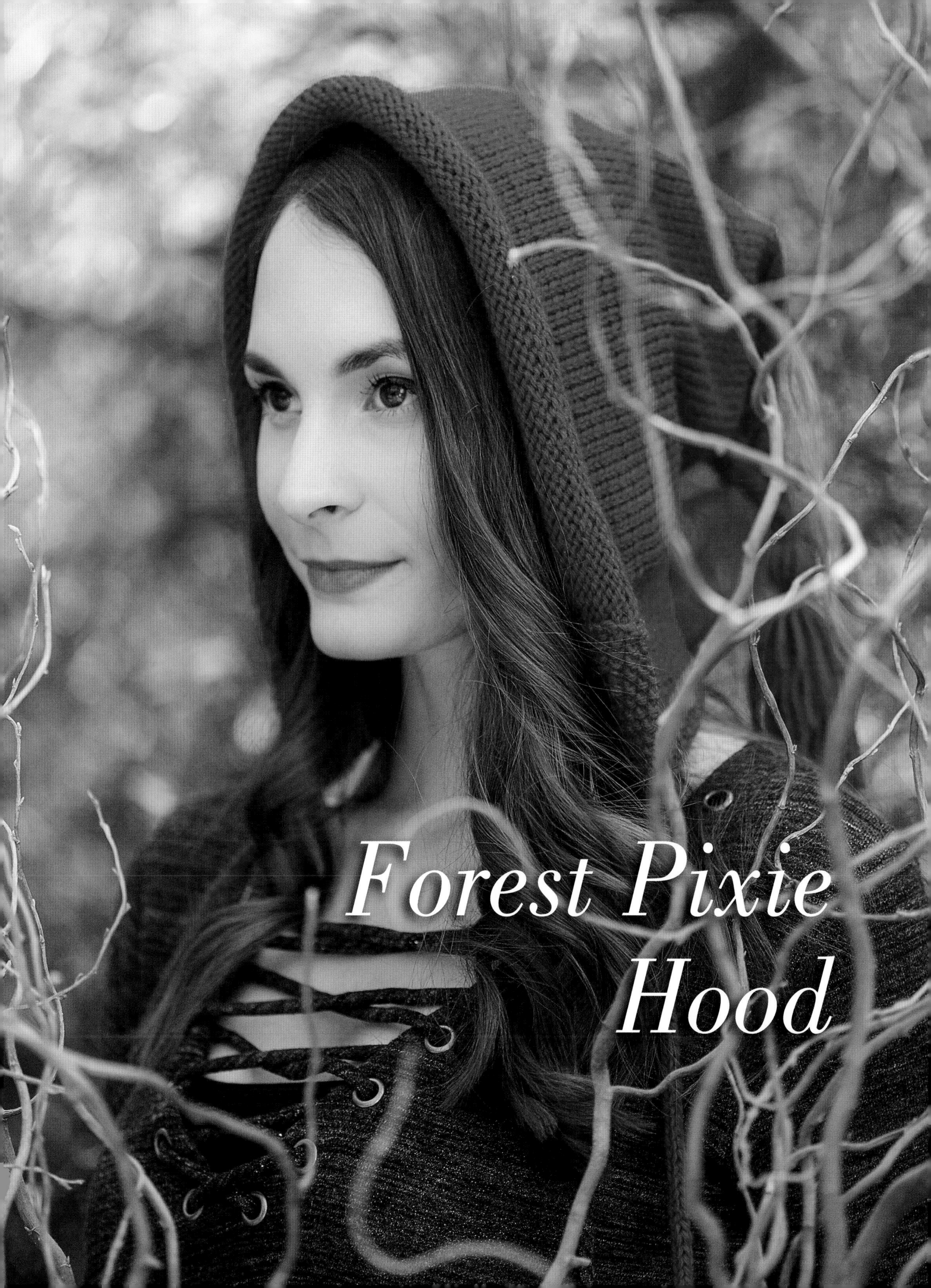

Forest Pixie Hood

This loom knit hood is both whimsical and practical. It's a little bit Red Riding Hood, wizard, and pixie in style. Perfect for festivals, Halloween, Christmas, and any other time you are feeling a bit romantic. It will keep your head warm and your hair intact—no hat hair with this lovely hood.

Level

Confident Beginner +

Finished Measurements

14 in/35.6 cm long x 18 in/45.7 cm front to back

Gauge

16 sts and 26 rows = 4 in/10.2 cm square in stockinette stitch

Yarn

Lion Brand Wool-Ease, worsted weight #4 (80% acrylic, 20% wool;197 yd/180 m, 3 oz/85 g per skein)
1 skein #138 Cranberry

Supplies

- 3/8 in/1 cm peg spacing round loom with 84 pegs
- Knitting tool
- Measuring tape
- Yarn/tapestry needle
- Crochet hook

Pattern Notes

- Top of hood is knit flat and then seamed.
- Stitches are later picked up along bottom edge of hood to work collar.
- The knitting at the front of the hood is designed to roll.
- For step-by-step instructions on picking up stitches and making I-cord, see pages 126–27.

Pattern

TOP OF HOOD

Foundation row: Chain CO 84 pegs; work as flat panel.
Rows 1–10: Knit.
Lift first row of sts up onto loom (just as you would for a hat brim), being careful to keep them aligned.
Row 11: Knit.
Rep row 11 until work measures 10 in/25.4 cm.

Begin Decreasing Hood

Row 1: K2tog, knit to last 2 sts, ssk.
Rep row 1 until there are 4 stitches left on the loom.
Next row: K2tog, k2.
Chain one bind-off.

Seam Hood

Using mattress stitch, fold hood in half and seam from narrowest point to where hood first started to decrease.

BASE OF HOOD

With right side facing out, place hood upside down through the loom. Begin picking up the edge stitches (last row of sts) and placing them on the loom. You will be knitting the collar of the hood for this portion. You may have to coax the stitches loose around the seam area. Lift the loom, look underneath and make sure there are no gaps and that all stitches have been placed on the loom in order. You are now ready to knit the collar.

Seed Stitch

Stitch count will vary, so follow the directions below for working the seed stitch collar.
Row 1: *K1, p1, rep from * to end (you may end with a p1 or k1, just stay in sequence, all rows).
Row 2: Purl the knits, knit the purls (from the last row).
Work in seed stitch until total length of hood measures 13½ in/34.3 cm.

I-Cord Tie

Next row: Continue in seed stitch for 3 pegs/sts, bind off all stitches until you reach the last 3 stitches, work I-cord tie over the last 3 sts, being careful not to drop the 3 sts at the start of the row. (You will work 2 ties on either side of the loom on remaining 6 pegs. Each tie will be worked over 3 pegs/sts.)
Row 1: Knit peg 1, knit peg 3, knit peg 2.
Rep row 1 until knitting measures 24 in/61 cm.
Next row: K2tog, ssk (1 stitch remains).
Bind off; leave a 5 in/12.7 cm tail.
Make fringe: Thread four 10 in/25.4 cm lengths of yarn through bottom of I-cord, pull them even, and tie them together to secure.
Rep above on other side of loom over remaining 3 pegs.

Finishing

Weave in ends. No blocking is needed.

Autumn
Gathering Scarf

Light and airy, this asymmetrical scarf features an easy eyelet lace along the edges and at the bottom of the scarf. A pocket gathers the scarf gently to the side. This is a lovely accent piece to jazz up any outfit.

Level

Intermediate

Finished Measurements

53¼ in/135.3 cm long x 13 in/33 cm wide

Gauge

18 sts and 34 rows = 4 in/10.2 cm square in stockinette stitch

Yarn

Lion Brand Shawl in a Ball, worsted weight #4 (58% cotton, 39% acrylic, 3% other fiber; 481 yd/440 m, 5.3 oz/150 g per skein)
1 skein #206 Peaceful Earth

Supplies

- ⅜ in/1 cm peg spacing loom using 58 pegs
- Knitting tool
- Crochet hook
- Tape measure

Pattern Notes

- Scarf is knit from top to bottom.
- Cast-on stitches are lifted to form pocket for gathering scarf (see page 125 for instructions on lifting stitches).

Pattern

POCKET

Foundation row: Chain CO 58 sts; work as flat panel.
Row 1: Knit.
Rep row 1 until knitting measures 6½ in/16.5 cm.
Reach down below each stitch and lift each stitch from the cast-on row up onto the loom, forming a pocket/hem.

BODY OF SCARF

Row 1: Knit. (58 sts)
Row 2: K1, p1, yo-k2tog, p1, knit to last 5 sts, p1, yo-k2tog, p1, k1.
Rows 3–5: K1, p1, k1, p1, knit to last 4 sts, p1, k1, p1, k1.
Row 6: K1, yo-p2tog, k1, yo-p2tog, knit to last 6 sts, yo-p2tog, k1, yo-p2tog, k1.
Rows 7–9: As rows 3–5.
Rep rows 2–9 until total work measures 50 in/127 cm.

LACE BORDER

Row 1: *K2, yo-k2tog, rep from * to last 2 sts, k2. (58 sts)
Rows 2–4: Knit.
Row 5: K2, *ssk-yo, k2, rep from * to end.
Rows 6–8: Knit.
Rows 9–24: Rep rows 1–8 (2 times).
Chain one bind-off.

Finishing

Weave in ends. Block scarf to open eyelets. Pull bind-off edge through pocket of scarf, being careful not to twist the knitting. Add 7 in/17.8 cm fringe to bottom of scarf.

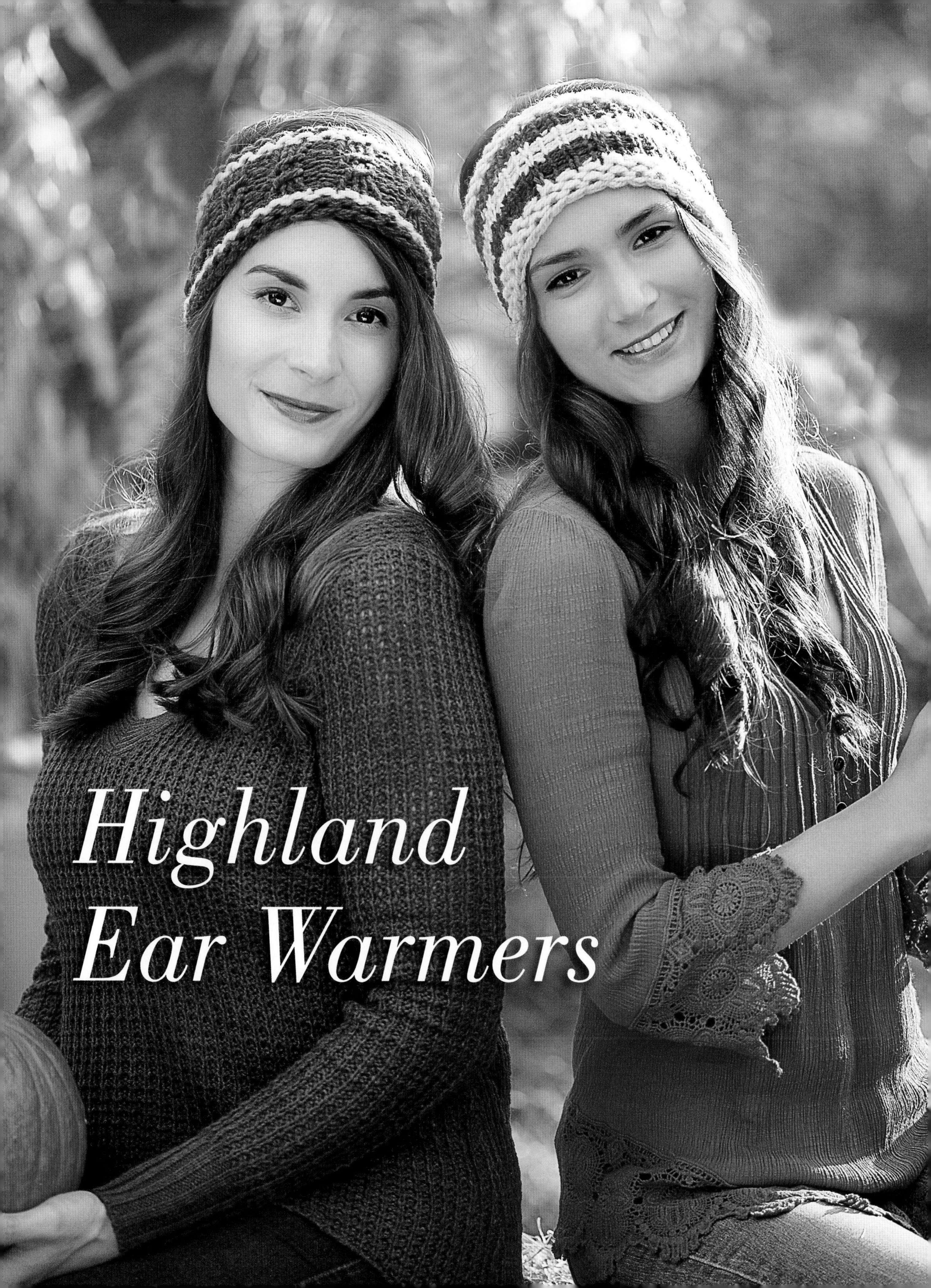

Highland Ear Warmers

The two versions of these ear warmers are a perfect way to familiarize yourself with locally farmed wool and indie dyers. Minimally processed wool and twisted and tuck stitches combine to give these ear warmers lovely texture and warmth. They make excellent gifts, as they can be knit in one evening!

Level

Confident Beginner

Finished Measurements

4½ in/11.4 cm high x 21 in/53.3 cm wide

Gauge

7 sts and 16 rows = 4 in/10.2 cm square in both mock cable and tuck stitch

Yarn

Swan Bay Farm Hand Dyed, worsted weight #4 (75% merino, 25% Lincoln/Cotswold cross; 144 yd/132 m, 4.3 oz/122 g per skein). Amounts below are enough to make both versions.
1 skein Cinnamon
1 skein Natural

Supplies

- ¾ in/2 cm peg spacing round loom with 36 pegs
- Knitting tool
- Crochet hook
- Stitch holder
- Tape measure
- Yarn/tapestry needle (for optional flower)
- Medium button (optional for flower)

Pattern Notes

- Ear warmers are knit in the round and are seamless.
- Warmer is knit from the bottom up.
- When looking for wool for this project, check out your local wool farmers and hand-dyed/natural wools to get the same look. Alternatively, there are many options to be found on the Internet.
- Because yarn weights can vary significantly from skein to skein, pay careful attention to gauge or use a tape measure to add/subtract rows as necessary to achieve proper sizing.
- When asked to CO1, use the true cable cast-on method as described on page 110.

Mock Cable Ear Warmer

SPECIAL STITCH

RTW (right twist): Place the stitch from peg 2 on a stitch holder. Pick up the stitch on peg 1 with your knitting tool and put it on peg 2. Transfer the stitch on the holder to peg 1. Knit pegs 1 and 2 as indicated in pattern. (See page 116 for photo-illustrated instructions.)

Pattern

Foundation row: Chain CO 36 sts with 2 strands MC; join to work in the round.

Row 1: Knit.
Row 2: Purl.
Change to CC but do not cut MC.
Row 3: Knit in CC.
Row 4: Purl in CC.
Cut CC and change to MC.
Row 5: Knit.
Rows 6–8: *K2, p1, rep from * to end of round (work row 8 loosely to allow for easier twisting of sts).
Row 9: *RTW, p1, rep from * to end of round.
Rows 10–13: Rep rows 6–9 (1 time).
Rows 14–16: Rep rows 6–8 (1 time).
Change to CC but do not cut MC.
Row 17: Knit.
Row 18: Purl.
Cut CC and change to MC.
Row 19: Knit.
Row 20: Purl.
Chain one bind-off. Weave in ends.

Tuck Stitch Ear Warmer

SPECIAL STITCH

Tuck1: Using the regular knit stitch, knit all sts on each peg together. This will tuck your skipped sts into this one stitch.

Pattern

Foundation round: Chain CO all sts with 2 strands MC.
Rnd 1: Knit.
Rnd 2: Purl.
Rnds 3–4: Rep rnds 1 and 2 (1 time).
Rnds 5–7 (in CC): *K2, skip1 wyif, rep from * to end of round.
Rnd 8 (in CC): *K2, Tuck1, rep from * to end of round.
Rnds 9–12: Rep rnds 5–8 in MC.
Rnds 13–16: Rep rnds 5–8 in CC.
Rnds 17–20: Rep rnds 1–4 in MC using 2 strands.
Chain one bind-off. Weave in ends.

Flower (optional)

Foundation row: Chain CO 4 pegs with 1 strand CC.
Rows 1–2: Knit.
Row 3: P2tog, purl 2.
Row 4: K3, cast on 1 st.
Row 5: Knit.
Row 6: Purl.
Row 7: K2tog, k2.
Row 8: K3, CO 1 st.
Row 9: Purl.
Rows 10–36: Rep rows 1–9 (3 times).
Bind off using gather method (see page 112), leaving a long tail for gathering and seaming. Weave the yarn tail in and out of each stitch on the straight edge of work and pull to gather. Seam the cast-on edge and bind-off edge together; use remaining yarn to sew button to the center of the flower.
Attach flower to the side of the ear warmer using a safety pin or sew to warmer permanently.

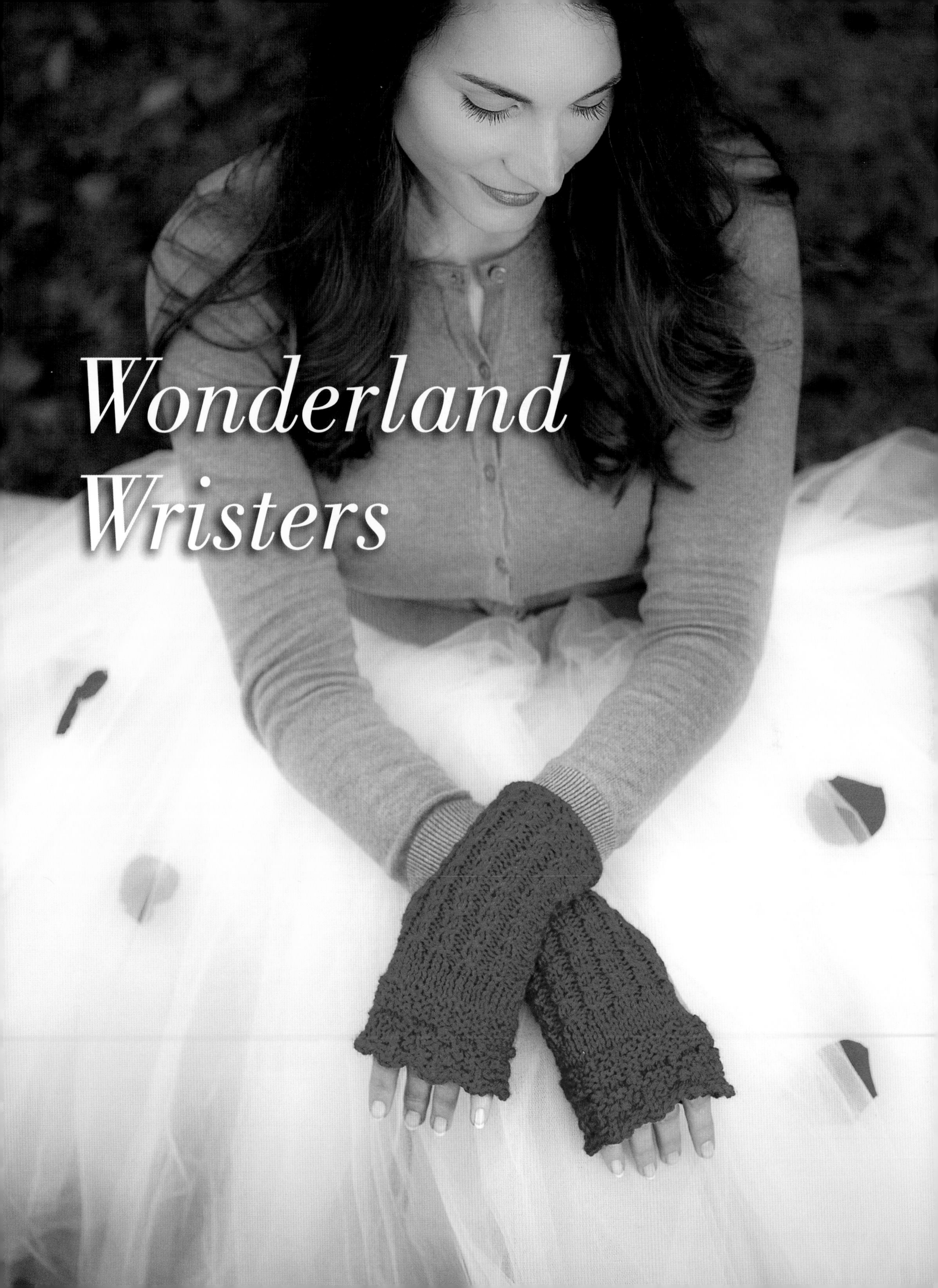

Wonderland Wristers

Romantic, Victorian-style wristers with a twisted cable ribbing and wide lace edging, these reading mitts will add the perfect touch to a pretty outfit while keeping your hands warm.

Level

Intermediate+

Finished Measurements

8½ in/21.6 cm long x 9½ in/24.1 cm circumference

Gauge

18 sts and 30 rows = 4 in/10.2 cm square in mock cable rib stitch

Yarn

Patons Classic Wool, worsted weight #4 (100% wool; 210 yd/192 m, 3.5 oz/100 g per skein)
1 skein #00230 Bright Red

Supplies

- ⅜ in/1 cm peg spacing round loom with 44 pegs
- Knitting tool
- Crochet hook
- Stitch holder
- Measuring tape
- Yarn/tapestry needle
- Cable needle (optional)

Special Stitches

MB (make bobble): Make an e-wrap knit stitch by making an e-wrap and lifting the bottom loop over the top wrap (you may wish to keep this stitch on a cable needle for easier lifting later). Make 4 more e-wrap knit stitches on the same peg. Reach down below the peg and pick up the first e-wrap knit stitch and lift it onto the peg. E-wrap knit all stitches on peg together as one.

LTW (left twist): Place the stitch from peg 1 on a stitch holder. Pick up the stitch on peg 2 with your knitting tool and put it on peg 1. Transfer the stitch on the holder to peg 2. Knit pegs 1 and 2 as indicated in the pattern.

Pattern Notes

- Mitt is knit flat and then seamed closed, leaving an opening for the thumb.
- When asked to CO1, use the true cable cast-on method as described on page 110.
- For photo-illustrated instructions on making a bobble and left twist (LTW), see pages 119–20 and 116.

Pattern (make 2)

Foundation row: Chain CO 44 sts; work as flat panel.
Row 1: Knit.
Row 2: K1, *psso, p2, rep from * to last 3 sts, yo-k2tog, k1.
Rows 3–4: Rep rows 1 and 2 (1 time).
Row 5: Knit.
Row 6: K1, *yo-p2tog, k1, rep from * to last peg, k1.
Row 7: Knit.
Decrease: Move the stitch from peg 6 to peg 7, peg 12 to peg 13, peg 18 to 19, peg 26 to 25, peg 32 to 31, peg 39 to peg 38. Pull bottom stitches over top stitches. Now move all sts evenly toward center, filling the gaps. Move the sts 1 peg at a time. (38 sts)
Row 8: K1, purl to last st, k1.
Row 9: Knit.
Row 10: *K3, MB, rep from * to last 2 sts, k2.
Row 11: Knit.
Row 12: As row 8.
Row 13: *K2, p2, rep from * to last 2 sts, k2.
Row 14: *P2, k2, rep from * to last 2 sts, p2.
Rows 15–18: Rep rows 13 and 14 (2 times).
Row 19: K2tog, knit to last 2 sts, ssk. (36 sts)
Row 20: Knit.
Rows 21–24: Rep rows 19 and 20 (2 times). (32 sts)
Row 25: Knit.
Row 26: *K2, p1, rep to last 2 sts, k2.
Row 27: CO1 st, *k2, p1, rep to last 2 sts, k2, CO1 stitch. Do not work cast-on sts on this row. (34 sts)
Row 28 (knit loosely): K3, *p1, k2, to last 4 sts, p1, k3.
Row 29: K1, *LTW, p1, rep from * to last 3 sts, LTW, k1.
Row 30: K3, *p1, k2, rep from * to last st, k1.
Row 31: K3, *p1, k2, rep from * to last st, k1.
Row 32 (knit loosely): K3, *p1, k2, rep from * to last st, k1.
Row 33: K1, *LTW, p1, rep from * to last 3 sts, LTW, k1.
Rep rows 30–33 until work measures 8¼ in/21 cm.
Next row: As row 30.
Chain one bind-off all sts, leaving a long tail for seaming closed the side of the mitt.

Finishing

Fold mitt in half with right side out. Seam mitt closed 4 in/10.2 cm from bottom, leave 1½ in/3.8 cm open for thumb, then seam to top, approximately 3 in/7.6 cm (see white dotted lines on illustration). Rep for second mitt. Weave in ends. Block lightly if desired.

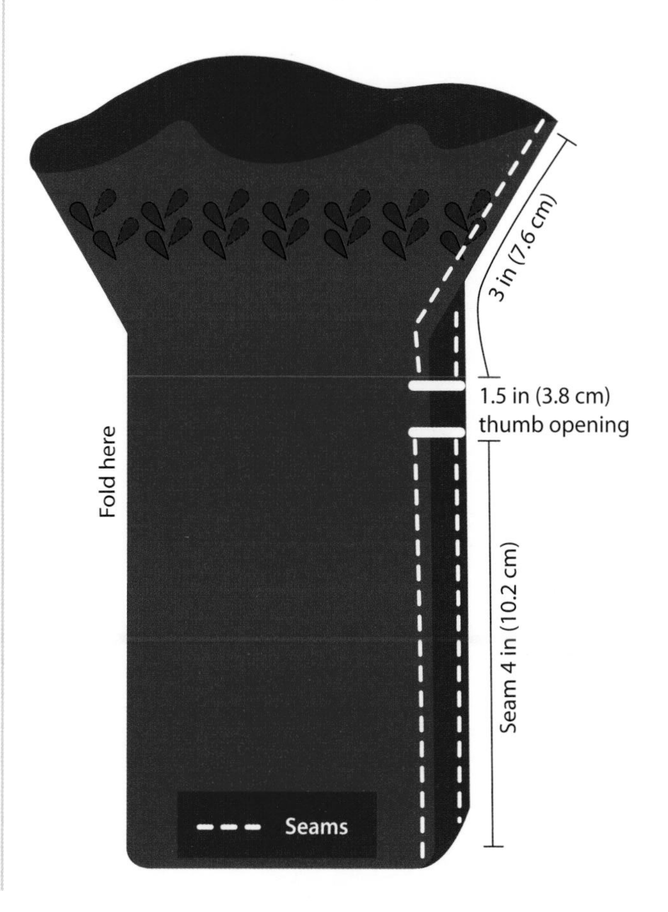

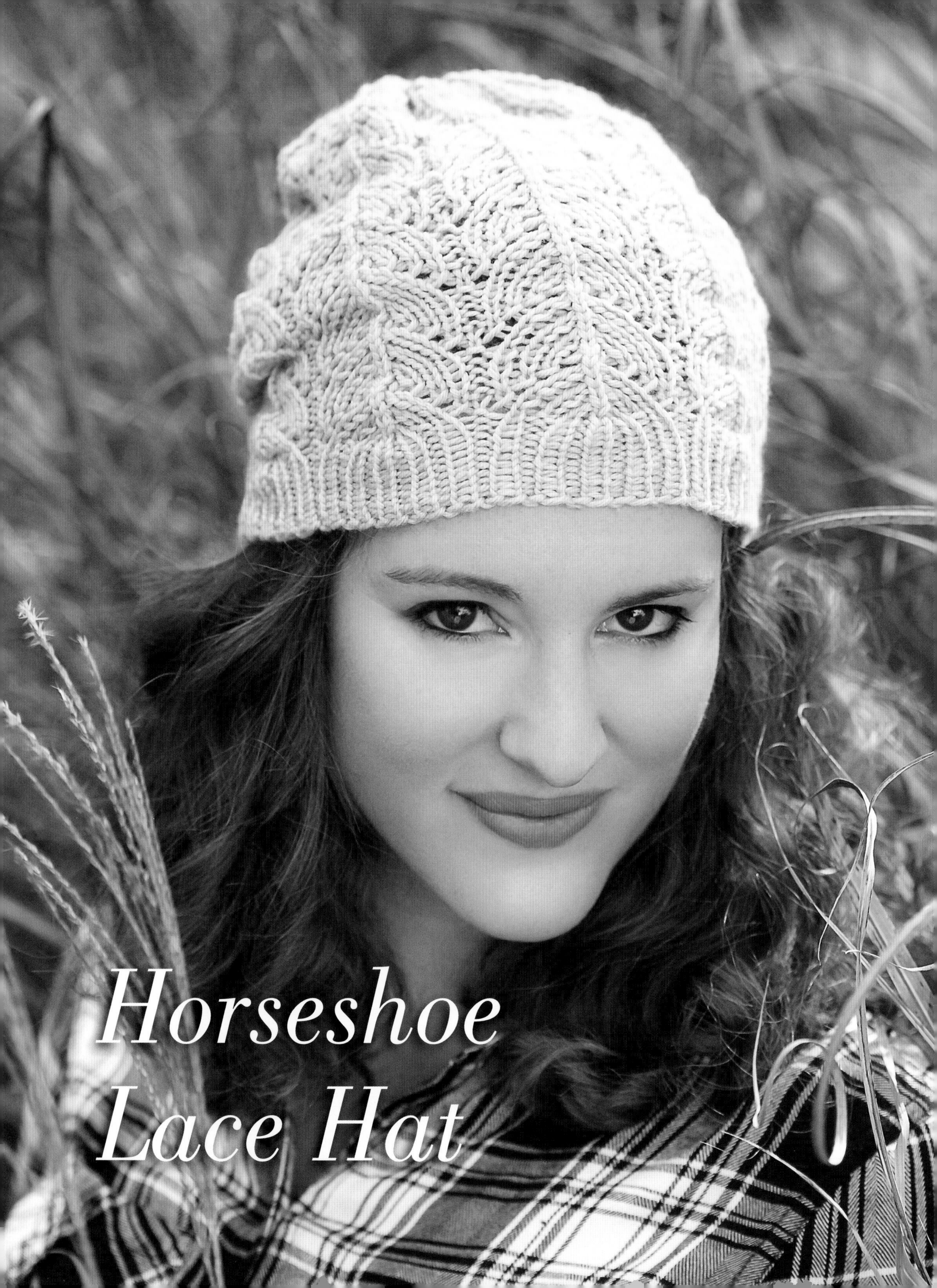

Horseshoe Lace Hat

This lightweight hat is adorned with a beautiful lace stitch pattern. Don't be intimidated by the stitchwork on this piece; after a few rows, you'll find that it's not as difficult as it looks!

Level

Advanced

Finished Measurements

9½ in/24.1 cm long x 21 in/53.3 cm circumference

Gauge

18 sts and 32 rows = 4 in/10.2 cm square in horseshoe lace stitch

Yarn

Knit Picks Swish Worsted, worsted weight #4 (100% superwash merino wool; 110 yd/100.5 m, 1.75 oz/50 g per skein)
2 skeins #25143 Cornmeal

Supplies

- ⅜ in/1 cm peg spacing round loom with 80 pegs
- Knitting tool
- Crochet hook
- Measuring tape
- Stitch markers (optional)

Special Abbreviations

cf: Count forward
mf: Move forward
mb: Move back
fg: Fill gap

Special Stitches

mb1-k: Move back one stitch, then knit this same stitch.
k3tog: Knit 3 stitches together on this peg using the regular knit stitch (k). In this pattern, these stitches will already be present on the peg due to the earlier movement of your stitches.

Pattern Notes

- Hat is worked in the round from the bottom up.
- For photo-illustrated instructions on counting forward (cf), moving forward (mf), moving back (mb), and filling gap (fg), see pages 123–24.
- You may wish to use stitch markers to mark the pattern repeat and help guide you while you work. Pattern stitch works in multiples of 10.
- When asked to fill gap (fg) in this pattern, you will move the stitches forward to make room for the yarn over.

Pattern

RIBBED BORDER

Foundation round: Chain CO 80 pegs; join to work in the round.

Rnds 1–12: *K1, p1, rep from * to end of round.

BODY OF HAT

Row 1: *Cf4-mf1, fg, yo, k3, cf2-mb1, k3tog, (mb1-k) 3 times, yo, k1, rep from * to end.

Row 2: Knit.

Row 3: *K1, cf3-mf1, fg, yo, k2, cf2-mb1, k3tog, (mb1-k) 2 times, yo, k1, p1, rep from * to end.

Row 4: *K9, p1, rep from * to end.

Row 5: *K2, cf2-mf1, fg, yo, k1, cf2-mb1, k3tog, mb1-k, yo, k2, p1, rep from * to end.

Row 6: As row 4.

Row 7: *K3, mf1, yo, cf2-mb1, k3tog, yo, k3, p1, rep from * to end.

Row 8: Knit.

Rep rows 1–8 (7 times or until hat measures 9½ in/24.1 cm).

Decrease stitches by moving the first stitch to the next peg and then pull the bottom loop over the top loop; rep all the way around the loom until half the stitches are decreased. Do not move your stitches inward as you do this.

Bind off remaining stitches using the gather method. Weave in ends and block hat if desired.

BODY OF HAT

Row												Row
8												
					O	⋀	O					7
6												
				O		⋀		O				5
4												
			O			⋀			O			3
2												
		O				⋀				O		1

10 st repeat

Symbol	Meaning
□	k
O	yo
⋀	psso/k3tog

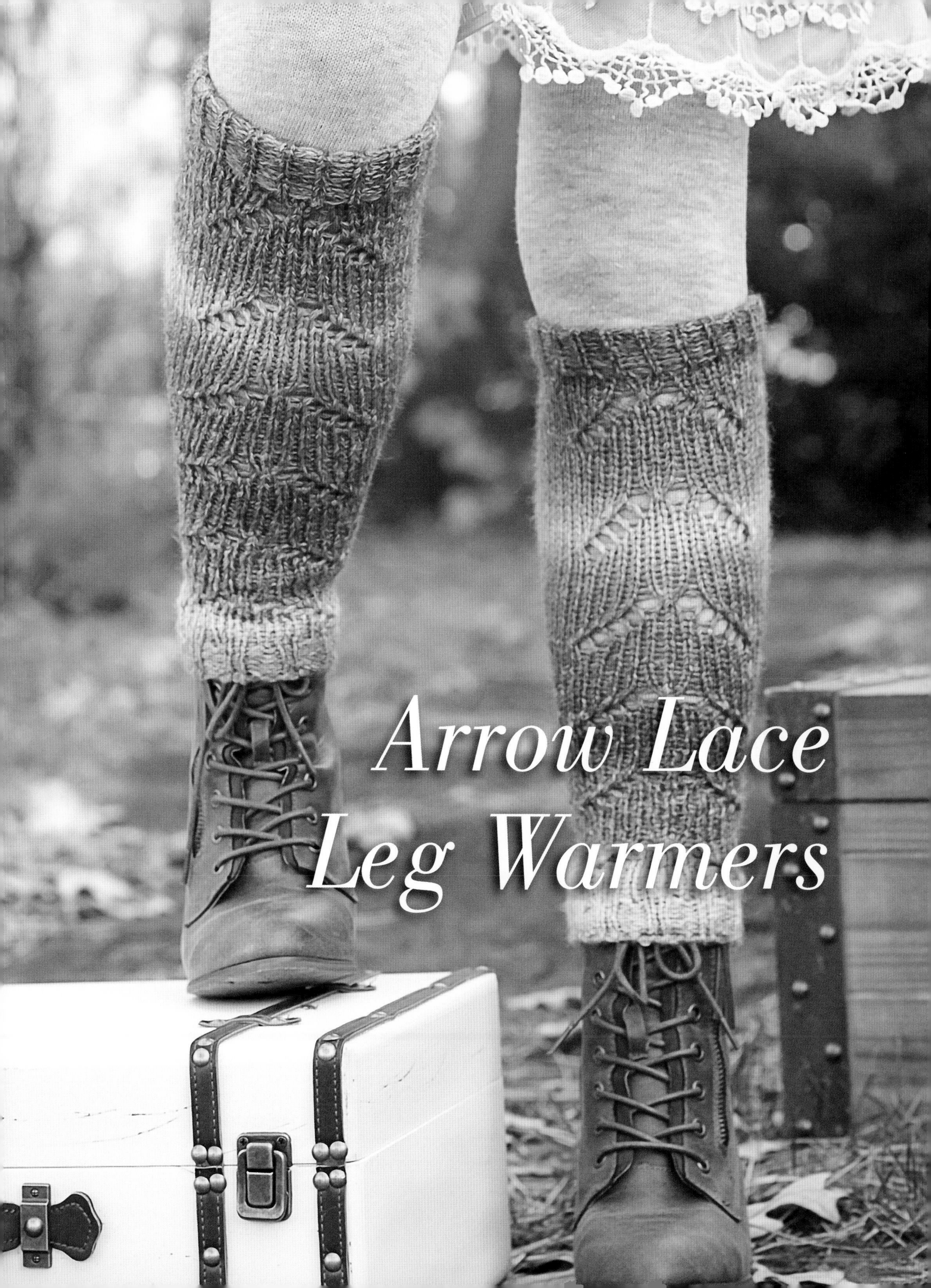

Arrow Lace Leg Warmers

A fitted, lace leg warmer perfect for wearing over leggings or skinny jeans.

Level

Intermediate

Finished Measurements

8½ in/21.6 cm at ankle, 14 in/35.6 cm around at calf, 15 in/38.1 cm long

Sized for ladies medium/teen. Size can be adjusted for width and length if needed.

Gauge

16 sts and 28 rows = 4 in/10.2 cm square in stockinette stitch

Yarn

Ella Rae Seasons, worsted weight #4 (76% acrylic, 14% wool, 10% polyamide; 219 yd/200 m, 3.5 oz/100 g per skein)

2 skeins #16

Supplies

- ⅜ in/1 cm peg spacing round loom with 60 pegs
- Knitting tool
- Measuring tape
- Yarn/tapestry needle
- 2 stitch markers

Pattern Notes

- Top of leg warmer is hemmed.
- Leg warmers are knit flat to allow for decreases.
- Place markers on pegs 25 and 36; arrow lace will be worked between these markers.
- For sizing convenience, arrow lace is indicated within brackets [ ]. If you would like to widen these leg warmers, just add the same number of stitches to either side of lace repeat as needed for fit. Similarly, you can make these narrower by deleting the same number of stitches on either side of the repeat. 4 sts should equal approximately 1 in/2.5 cm if meeting gauge. Move stitch markers to mark the center 12 sts where you will work the lace repeat.

Pattern

RIBBING

Foundation row: Chain CO 60 pegs.
Row 1: *K1, p1, rep from * to end of row.
Row 2: *P1, k1, rep from * to end of row.
Rows 3–20: Rep rows 1 and 2 (9 times).
Pick up sts from cast-on row and place them up on the loom, being careful to keep the sts in line with the correct peg. Knit row 21 loosely to preserve stretch.
Rows 21–23: Knit.

BODY OF LEG WARMER: ARROW LACE

Row 1: Knit to 1st marker, [k4, yo-k2tog, ssk-yo, k4], knit to end of rnd.
Row 2: Knit.
Row 3: Knit to 1st marker, [k3, yo-k2tog, k2, ssk-yo, k3], knit to end of rnd.
Row 4: Knit.
Row 5: Knit to 1st marker, [k2, yo-k2tog, k4, ssk-yo, k2], knit to end of rnd.
Row 6: Knit.
Row 7: Knit to 1st marker, [k1, yo-k2tog, k6, ssk-yo, k1], knit to end of rnd.
Row 8: Knit.
Row 9: Knit to 1st marker, [yo-k2tog, k8, ssk-yo], knit to end of rnd.
Rows 10–14: Knit.
Rows 15–42: Rep rows 1–14 (2 times).

Begin decreasing leg warmer (decrease to 34 sts; adjust this if necessary for fit).
Row 1: Knit to 1st marker, [k4, yo-k2tog, ssk-yo, k4], knit to end of rnd.
Row 2: K2tog, knit to last 2 sts, ssk.
Row 3: Knit to 1st marker, [k3, yo-k2tog, k2, ssk-yo, k3], knit to end of rnd.
Row 4: K2tog, knit to last 2 sts, ssk.
Row 5: Knit to 1st marker, [k2, yo-k2tog, k4, ssk-yo, k2], knit to end of rnd.
Row 6: K2tog, knit to last 2 sts, ssk.
Row 7: Knit to 1st marker, [k1, yo-k2tog, k6, ssk-yo, k1], knit to end of rnd.
Row 8: K2tog, knit to last 2 sts, ssk.
Row 9: Knit to 1st marker, [yo-k2tog, k8, ssk-yo], knit to end of rnd.
Row 10: K2tog, knit to last 2 sts, ssk.
Row 11: Knit.
Rows 12–13: Rep rows 10 and 11 (1 time).
Row 14: K2tog, knit to last 2 sts, ssk.
Rep rows 1–14 until there are 34 sts left on the loom. Stop decreasing and work as for main leg warmer until total knitting measures 14 in/35.6 cm (or desired length less 1 in/2.5 cm for bottom ribbing).

BOTTOM RIBBING

Row 1: *K2, p2, rep from * to end of row.
Rep row 1 until ribbing measures 1 in/2.5 cm.
Bind off loosely using chain one method, being careful to preserve stretch.

Finishing

Weave in ends. Seam edges together using mattress stitch. Block lightly to open eyelets.

ARROW LACE (worked between markers)

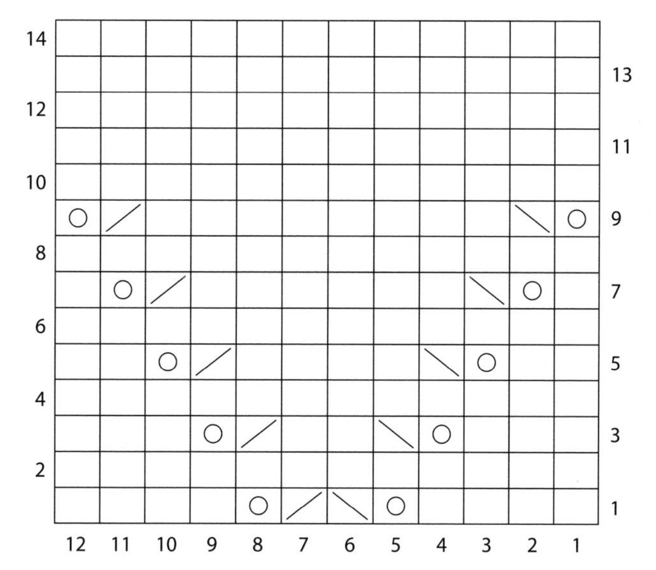

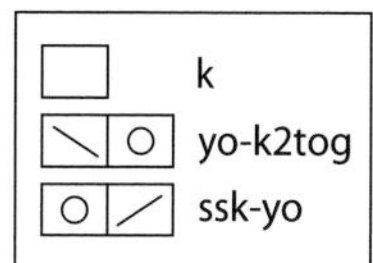

Retro Tube Socks

Feminine meets sporty in these retro, easy-knit, knee-high tube socks. Since they are knit as a tube, no heel is required. Wet blocking is used after finishing to widen the calf area.

Level

Confident Beginner+

Finished Measurements

20 in/50.8 cm long x 10 in/25.4 cm circumference (length is adjustable)

To fit adult ladies, medium width.

Gauge

20 sts and 36 rows = 4 in/10.2 cm square in stockinette stitch

Yarn

West Yorkshire Spinners 100% Bluefaced Leicester, DK weight #3 (100% wool; 122 yd/112 m, 1.76 oz/50 g per skein)
  1 skein #542 Coral (MC)

Berroco Ultra Wool, DK weight #3 (100% superwash wool; 292 yd/267 m, 3.5 oz/100 g per skein)
  1 skein #8301 Cream (CC)

Supplies

- ⅜ in/1 cm peg spacing round loom with 40 pegs
- Knitting tool
- Measuring tape
- Crochet hook

Pattern Notes

- Socks are knit from the toe up.
- Socks are knit as a tube, without heel.
- Socks are not increased at the calf; you will need to wet block the wool to create ease in this area. If you have a large/wide calf, then you may wish to work a shorter sock.
- Bottom half of the sock is u-knit; then you will switch to the regular knit stitch, as it has less tension for the wider calf area.
- Top of sock is hemmed to hide extra-stretchy bind-off, as this bind-off can look loose.
- For photo-illustrated instructions on the Kitchener cast-on, u-knit stitch, wrap and turn (w&t), and extra-stretchy bind-off, see pages 110–11, 114, 117, and 113.

Pattern

TOE/HEEL

Kitchener cast-on all 40 pegs in CC.

Foundation round: K40 (use regular knit stitch to lock in cast-on).

Decrease Toe (worked flat)

Begin decreasing toe, working over 20 pegs using short rows, using u-knit from now on.

Row 1: U-k19, w&t next peg.
Row 2: U-k18, w&t next peg.
Row 3: U-k17, w&t next peg.
Row 4: U-k16, w&t next peg.
Row 5: U-k15, w&t next peg.
Row 6: U-k14, w&t next peg.
Row 7: U-k13, w&t next peg.
Row 8: U-k12, w&t next peg.
Row 9: U-k11, w&t next peg.
Row 10: U-k10, w&t next peg (5 wraps on either side of toe/heel).

Begin increasing toe, working wraps as you come to them.

Row 11: U-k to the 1st wrapped peg, pick up wraps by knitting sts together, turn.

Row 12: Rep row 11; do not u-k the 1st st in the row (or last st knit in row 11).

Rep rows 11 and 12 until you've picked up the last wrapped peg on both sides of the toe, w&t the next peg.

Last row of increase: U-k to end of row.

SOCK BODY

Begin working in the round using MC.

Rnd 1: U-k.

Rep rnd 1 until total work measures 9½ in/24.1 cm. Close toe before measuring (see Kitchener Cast-on on pages 110–11 for how to close toe).

Next round: Knit (use regular knit st).

Continue last rnd until total work measure 17½ in/44.5 cm.

TOP STRIPING

Rnds 1–4: Knit in CC.
Rnds 5–6: Knit in MC.
Rnds 7–10: Knit in CC.
Rnds 11–12: Knit in MC.

TOP RIBBING

Rnds 1–20: *K1, p1, rep from * to end of round.

Lift stitches from 1st row of ribbing forming a hem. Alternatively, you can hem the sock with a yarn/tapestry needle after removing it from the loom.

Bind off using x-stretchy bind-off method or chain one bind-off.

Finishing

Weave in all ends. If the calf section of sock is too tight for your leg, wet block knitting to desired measurements. Do not overstretch knitting. Be careful to preserve ribbing.

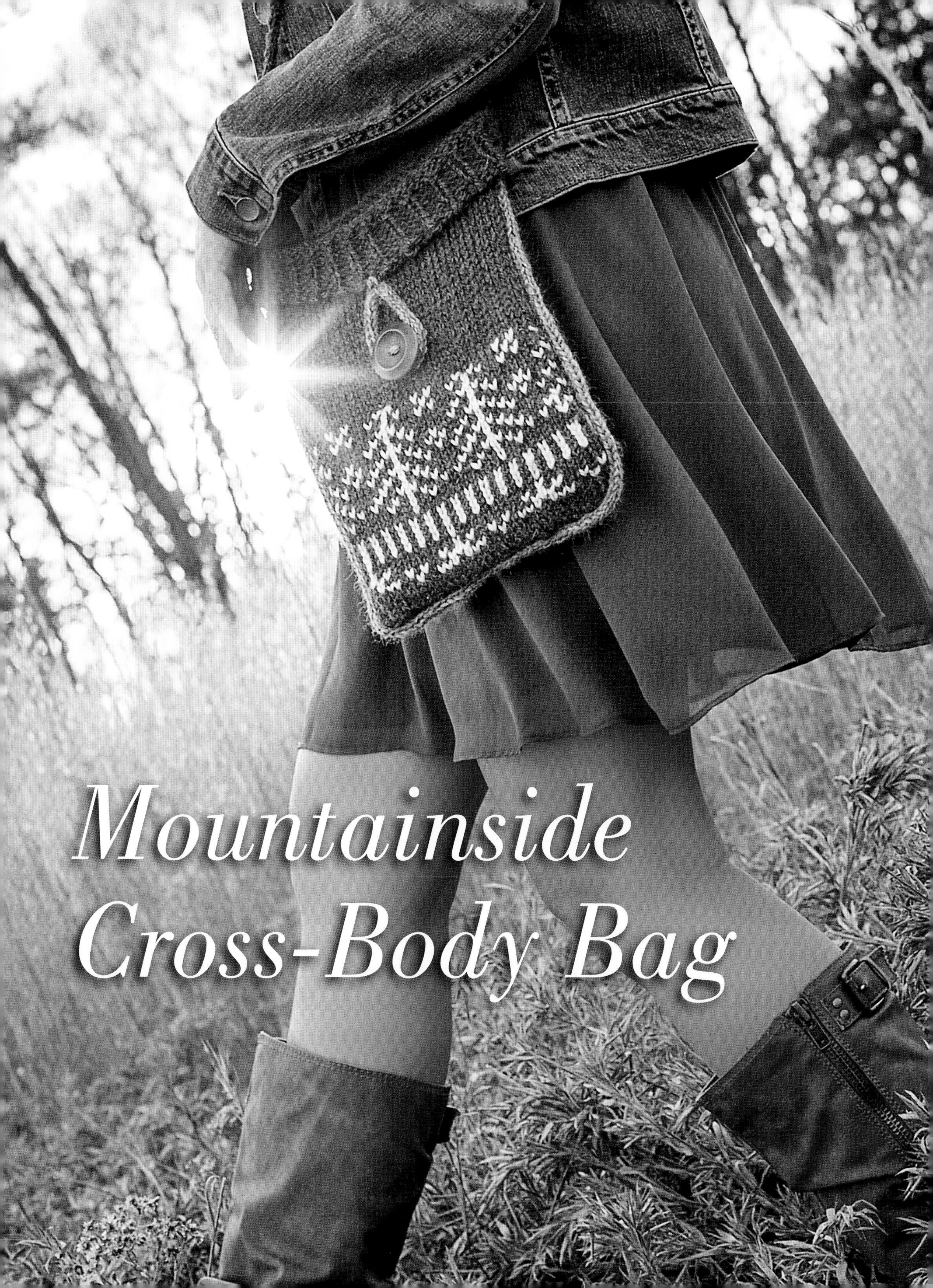

Mountainside Cross-Body Bag

If you're a country girl at heart, then this cross-body bag is perfect for holding all your essentials. It has an original Fair Isle design and long strap for a secure fit across the body.

Level

Confident Beginner

Finished Measurements

8 in/20.3 cm x 10 in/25.4 cm, not including strap

Gauge

18 sts and 28 rows = 4 in/10.2 cm square in stockinette stitch

Yarn

The Ross Farm Heritage & Rare Breed Fibers 100% Undyed Wool (250 yd/228.6 m). See below for ply and wool content.

Natural Dark Charcoal (Dark Brown), Warwick, Cotswold Wool, 3-ply worsted (A)

Natural Creamy White, Shetland Wool, 3-ply worsted (B)

Warm Moorit Brown (Medium Brown), Andy, Cotswold Wool, 2-ply sport (C)

Supplies

- ⅜ in/1 cm peg spacing round or adjustable loom with 72 pegs
- Knitting tool
- Crochet hook
- Measuring tape
- Yarn/tapestry needle
- 1 large wood button

Pattern Notes

- The bag is worked in the round and then seamed closed at the bottom.
- Use the regular knit stitch throughout pattern to keep your Fair Isle stitches looking their best.
- The wool used in this bag is undyed and in its natural state; therefore, colors will vary.
- For photo-illustrated instructions on working Fair Isle colorwork and making I-cord, see pages 126 and 127.

Pattern

Foundation round: Chain CO 72 pegs with 1 strand Color A; join to work in the round.
Rnds 1–8: *K2, p1, rep from * to end of round.
Rnds 9–47: Knit.

BEGIN FAIR ISLE PATTERN

If you prefer to work from a chart, see page 30.

Rnd 1: *K2 in A, k1 in B, k1 in A, [k1 in A, k3 in B] twice, rep from * to end of round.
Rnd 2: *[K1 in A, k1 in B] twice, k3 in A, k3 in B, k2 in A, rep from * to end of round.
Rnd 3: *K6 in A, [k1 in B, k1 in A] 3 times, rep from * to end of round.
Rnd 4: *K8 in A, k1 in B, k3 in A, rep from * to end of round.
Rnd 5: Knit in A.
Rnds 6–9: [K1 in B, k1 in A] 6 times, rep from * to end of round.
Rnd 10: Knit in A.
Rnd 11: *K5 in A, k1 in B, k6 in A, rep from * to end of round.
Rnd 12: *[K2 in A, k1 in B] 3 times, k3 in A, rep from * to end of round.
Rnd 13: *K1 in B, k2 in A, [k1 in B, k1 in A] 3 times, k1 in A, k1 in B, k1 in A, rep from * to end of round.
Rnd 14: *K1 in A, k1 in B, k2 in A, k2 in B, [k1 in B, k2 in A] twice, rep from * to end of round.
Rnd 15: *[K2 in A, k1 in B] 3 times, k3 in A, rep from * to end of round.
Rnd 16: *K2 in A, [k1 in A, k1 in B] 3 times, k4 in A, rep from * to end of round.
Rnd 17: *K1 in A, k1 in B, k2 in A, k2 in B, [k1 in B, k2 in A] twice, rep from * to end of round.
Rnd 18: *[K2 in A, k1 in B] 4 times, rep from * to end of round.
Rnd 19: *K1 in B, k2 in A, [k1 in B, k1 in A] 3 times, k1 in A, k1 in B, k1 in A, rep from * to end of round.
Rnd 20: *K4 in A, k3 in B, k4 in A, k1 in B, rep from * to end of round.
Rnd 21: *[K2 in A, k1 in B] 3 times, k3 in A, rep from * to end of round.
Rnd 22: *K2 in A, [k1 in A, k1 in B] 3 times, k4 in A, rep from * to end of round.
Rnd 23: *K4 in A, k3 in B, k5 in A, rep from * to end of round.
Rnd 24: *K1 in B, k1 in A, [k3 in A, k1 in B, k1 in A] twice, rep from * to end of round.
Rnd 25: *K3 in A, [k1 in B, k1 in A] 3 times, k2 in A, k1 in B, rep from * to end of round.

Rnd 26: *K1 in B, k3 in A, k3 in B, k3 in A, k1 in B, k1 in A, rep from * to end of round.
Rnd 27: *K5 in A, k1 in B, k6 in A, rep from * to end of round.
Cut Color B. Work in Color A only.
Rnds 28–35: Knit.
Chain one bind-off, leaving a long tail for seaming bottom of bag.

Finishing

Make a 3-stitch I-cord 42 in/106.7 cm long for strap in Color A. Using mattress stitch, close the bottom of the bag. Fold the top of the bag down approximately 1½ in/3.8 cm, just below ribbing, forming a cuff. Measure around your bag from the bottom of the cuff to the other side. Make a 3-stitch I-cord in Color C the length of this measurement. Sew the I-cord to the bag, attaching it to the cuff. This will hold the cuff in place. Make a 6 in/15.25 cm, 3-stitch I-cord in Color A and attach ends, forming a loop. Attach to center front of the bag. Align the button with the I-cord loop and sew to the bag. See illustration on page 30.

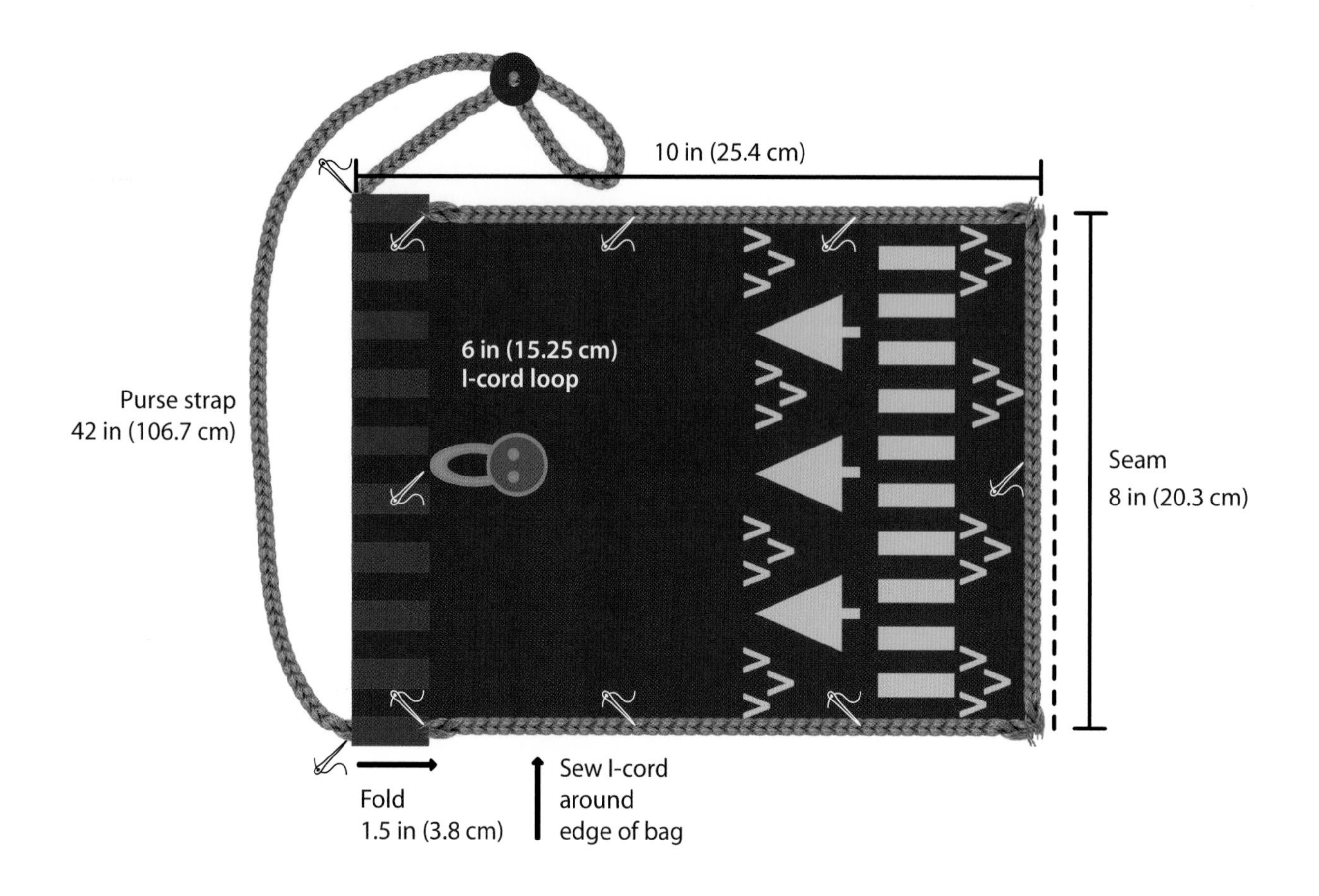
10 in (25.4 cm)
6 in (15.25 cm)
I-cord loop
Purse strap
42 in (106.7 cm)
Seam
8 in (20.3 cm)
Fold
1.5 in (3.8 cm)
Sew I-cord
around
edge of bag

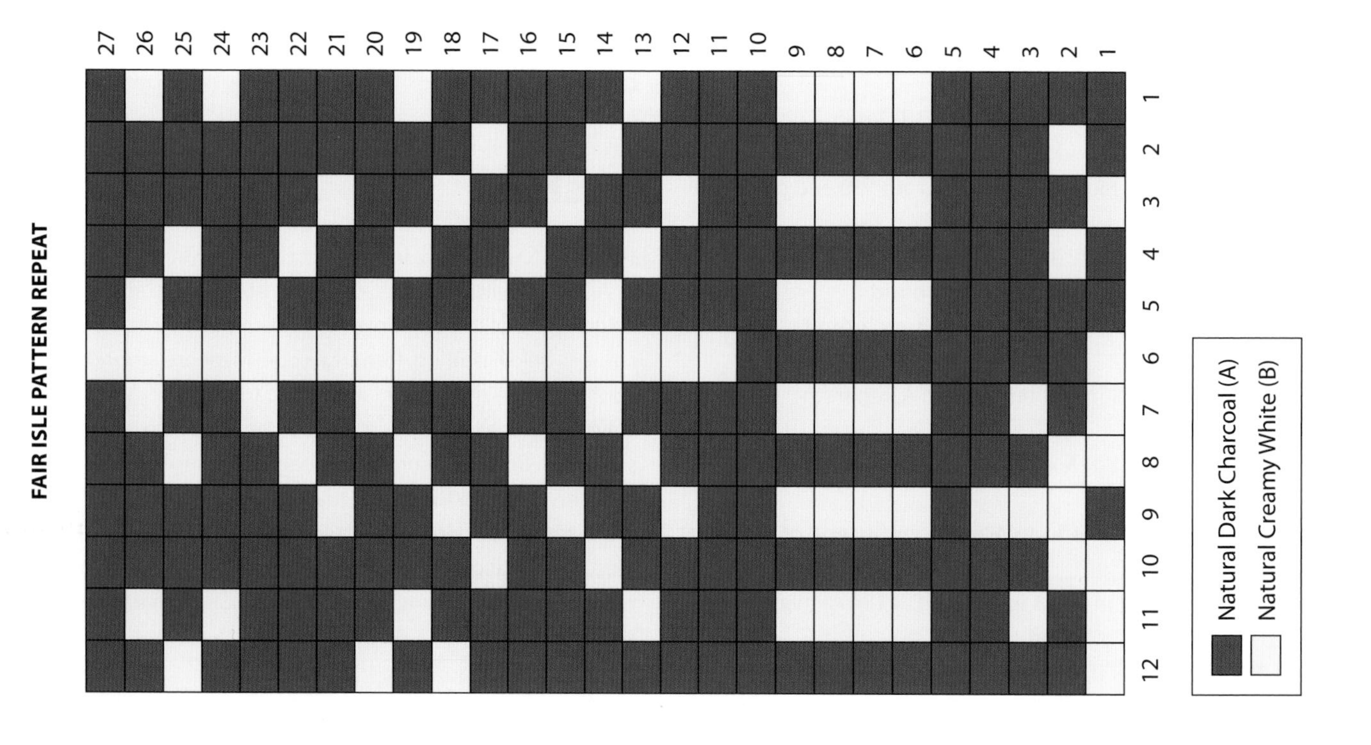
FAIR ISLE PATTERN REPEAT
Natural Dark Charcoal (A)
Natural Creamy White (B)

Eyelet Shawl

Symmetrical eyelets are worked both horizontally and vertically along this wrap. The diagonal edging gives added detail and eliminates the need for purl stitches. Worked in a worsted weight wool, this shawl is both warm and elegant.

Level

Confident Beginner

Finished Measurements

14 in/35.6 cm wide x 64 in/162.6 cm long

Gauge

18 sts and 24 rows = 4 in/10.2 cm square in stockinette stitch

Yarn

Patons Classic Wool Worsted, worsted weight #4 (100% wool; 210 yd/192 m, 3.5 oz/100 g per skein)
4 skeins #00201 Winter White

Supplies

- ⅜ in/1 cm peg spacing loom with 60 pegs
- Knitting tool
- Crochet hook
- Stitch markers
- Measuring tape
- Yarn/tapestry needle (optional)

Special Stitches

sh3-yo (shift 3, yarn over): Takes place over the first 4 stitches at the beginning of a row, shifting 3 stitches toward the outside edge. Move the stitch from peg 2 to peg 1. Move the stitch from peg 3 to peg 2. Move the stitch from peg 4 to peg 3. Knit 2 together on peg 1, knit pegs 2 and 3, e-wrap peg 4 (yarn over) but do not knit.

yo-sh3 (yarn over, shift 3): Takes place over the last 4 stitches of a row, shifting toward the outside edge. Move the stitch from peg 3 to peg 4, the outside peg. Move the stitch from peg 2 to peg 3. Move the stitch from peg 1 to peg 2. E-wrap peg 1 (yarn over) but do not knit, knit pegs 2 and 3, knit 2 together on peg 4.

Pattern Notes

- Shawl is worked flat in one piece.
- You may use the u-knit or regular knit where knit (k) is indicated. The u-knit is a smaller stitch, so the shawl will be slightly smaller in measurement if using this stitch. Complete a gauge swatch using the u-knit to determine final sizing if you would like to use this stitch.
- Included are instructions for either a ribbed border or a hem at the beginning and end of this shawl. Hemmed border is shown in sample.
- Blocking is recommended to open eyelets and even out stitches.
- For photo-illustrated instructions on how to work sh3-yo and yo-sh3, and how to insert a lifeline, see pages 118–19 and 130.

Pattern

BORDER

Foundation row: Chain CO 60 pegs; work as flat panel.

If doing a ribbed border:

Row 1: *K1, p1, rep from * to end of row.
Row 2: *P1, k1, rep from * to end of row.
Rows 3–6: Rep rows 1–2 (2 times).

If working a hem:

Row 1: Knit.
Rep row 1 until work measures 2 in/5.1 cm. Lift the 1st row of sts up onto loom, one by one, forming hem. Take care to keep sts straight. Pull bottom loops over top loops.

BODY OF SHAWL

Row 1: Knit.
Row 2: Sh3-yo, knit to last 4 sts in row, yo-sh3.
Rows 3–4: Knit.
Rows 5–10: Rep rows 2–4 (2 times).
Row 11: Sh3-yo, k2, *yo-k2tog, k1, rep from * to last 6 sts, k2, yo-sh3.
Rep rows 2–11 until wrap measures 62 in/157.5 cm.

BORDER

If doing a ribbed border:

Row 1: *K1, p1, rep from * to end of row.
Row 2: *P1, k1, rep from * to end of row.
Rows 3–6: Rep rows 1–2 (2 times).

If working a hem:

Row 1: Knit (use a few st markers to mark this row for easier lifting or add a lifeline).

Knit 2 in/5.1 cm (make sure row numbers are equal to your first hem). Lift all sts from row 1 onto the loom, one by one, keeping your sts straight. Pull bottom loops over top loops. Bind off all stitches using your preferred method (bind-off will be hidden). (Alternatively, you can bind off without pulling up the sts and sew hem with a yarn/tapestry needle.)

Finishing

Weave in ends. If you made hems on the ends, you may close hem ends by using mattress stitch. Block wrap to open up eyelets.

Fair Isle Toque

Everyone needs a casual and sporty winter beanie. If you're new to colorwork, then this pattern is a wonderful introduction to Fair Isle knitting. It has an easy-to-memorize color pattern with no need to manage the floats.

Level

Beginner

Finished Measurements

8½ in/21.6 cm x 21 in/53.3 cm circumference

Gauge

13 sts and 22 rows = 4 in/10 cm square in stockinette stitch

Yarn

Patons Classic Wool Bulky, bulky weight #5 (100% wool; 78 yd/71 m, 3.5 oz/100 g per skein)
1 skein #89008 Aran (A)

Patons Classic Wool Worsted, worsted weight #4 (100% wool; 210 yd/192 m, 3.5 oz/100 g per skein)
1 skein #77115 New Denim (B)

Plymouth Yarn Homestead, Aran weight #4 (100% Peruvian Highland Wool; 191 yd/175 m, 3.5 oz/100 g per skein)
1 skein #7 Citron (C)

Plymouth Yarn Homestead, Aran weight #4 (100% Peruvian Highland Wool; 191 yd/175 m, 3.5 oz/100 g per skein)
1 skein #14 Dark Carnation (D)

Supplies

- ⅝ in/1.6 cm peg spacing round loom with 48 pegs
- Knitting tool
- Crochet hook
- Measuring tape
- Cardboard or pom-pom maker

Pattern Notes

- Loom friendly! This hat pattern is easily adapted to any loom with an even number of pegs. Just use appropriate size loom and yarn.
- Due to the stranding with Fair Isle, this hat has less stretch, making gauge important for fit. Take the time to check your gauge.
- For photo-illustrated instructions on how to work Fair Isle colorwork and the gather method of binding off, see pages 126 and 112.

Pattern

Foundation round: Chain CO all pegs with 1 strand A; join to work in the round.
Rnds 1–8: *K1, p1, rep from * to end of round.
Rnds 9–11: Knit.

BEGIN FAIR ISLE PATTERN

Rnd 1: *K1 in B, k1 in A, rep from * to end of round.
Rnd 2: *K1 in A, k1 in B, rep from * to end of round.
Cut A, work in B.
Rnd 3: Knit all sts in B.
Rnd 4: *K1 in C, k1 in B, rep from * to end of round.
Rnd 5: *K1 in B, k1 in C, rep from * to end of round.
Cut B, work in C.
Rnd 6: Knit all sts in C.
Rnd 7: *K1 in D, k1 in C, rep from * to end of round.
Rnd 8: *K1 in C, k1 in D, rep from * to end of round.
Cut C, work in D.
Rnd 9: Knit all sts in D.
Rnd 10: *K1 in A, k1 in D, rep from * to end of round.
Rnd 11: *K1 in D, k1 in A, rep from * to end of round.
Cut D, work in A.
Rnd 12: Knit all sts in A.
End first Fair Isle pattern; rep rnd 9 until hat measures 6½ in/16.5 cm.

BEGIN CROWN FAIR ISLE PATTERN

Rnd 1: *K1 in B, k1 in A, rep from * to end of round.
Rnd 2: *K1 in A, k1 in B, rep from * to end of round.
Cut A, work in B.
Rnd 3: Knit all sts in B.
Rep rnd 3 until hat measures 8½ in/21.6 cm.
Bind off using gather method.

Finishing

Weave in ends and make a 4 in/10.2 cm pom-pom for top of hat.

FAIR ISLE PATTERN

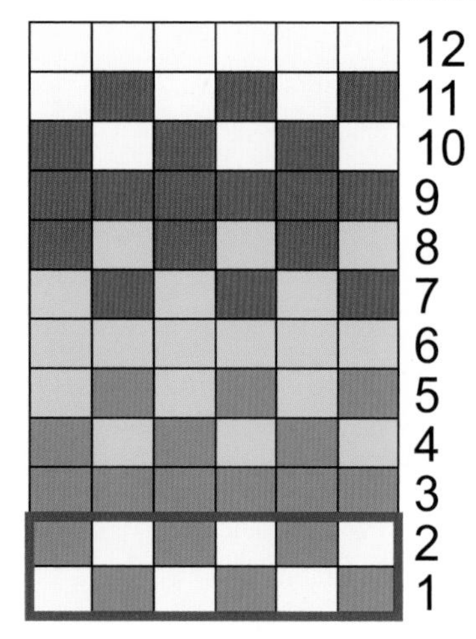

Yarn
Aran (A)
New Denim (B)
Citron (C)
DK Carnation (D)

Borders
Crown Repeat

Gothic Lattice Hat

A lattice design of twisting stitches stands out on a background of purls, recalling the vines on a gothic wall. This hat is lightweight and unisex, perfect for wearing indoors and out on blustery days.

Level

Intermediate

Finished Measurements

9 in/22.9 cm x 21 in/53.3 cm circumference
To fit teen/adult.

Gauge

16 sts and 30 rows = 4 in/10.2 cm square in gothic lattice stitch. Take time to check gauge.

Yarn

Knit Picks Swish Worsted, worsted weight #4 (100% superwash merino wool; 110 yd/100.5 m, 1.75 oz/50 g per skein)
2 skeins #25153 Marble Heather

Supplies

- 3/8 in/1 cm peg spacing round loom with 80 pegs
- Knitting tool
- Crochet hook
- Stitch holders
- Measuring tape
- Cable needle
- Stitch markers

Special Stitches

RTW (right twist): Place the stitch from peg 2 on a stitch holder. Pick up the stitch on peg 1 with your knitting tool and put it on peg 2. Transfer the stitch on the holder to peg 1. Knit pegs 1 and 2 as indicated in pattern.

LTW (left twist): Place the stitch from peg 1 on a stitch holder. Pick up the stitch on peg 2 with your knitting tool and put it on peg 1. Transfer the stitch on the holder to peg 2. Knit pegs 1 and 2 as indicated in the pattern.

Pattern Notes

- Hat is knit from the bottom up.
- Stitch chart works in multiples of 8 sts. Occasionally the stitch pattern will straddle rounds; this will be indicated within the pattern.
- Place a stitch marker every 8 pegs to help keep your bearings while working this pattern.
- For photo-illustrated instructions on working RTW and LTW and the gather method of binding off, see pages 116 and 112.

Pattern

Foundation round: Chain CO 80 pegs; join to work in the round.

RIBBED BAND

Rnds 1–8: *K1, p1, rep from * to end of round.

PATTERN STITCH

Rnd 1: [P6, k2] 10 times.
Rnd 2: [P6, RTW] 10 times.
Rnds 3–5: [P6, k2] 10 times.
Rnds 6–9: Rep rnds 2–5.
Rnd 10: [P6, RTW] 10 times.
Rnd 11: [P6, k2] 10 times.
Rnd 12: Skip1 wyib, [p4, LTW, RTW] 9 times, p4, LTW, RTW (RTW will take place on 1st peg of the next round).
Rnd 13: K1, P4, k1, [p2, k1, p4, k1] 9 times, p1 (this row begins on peg 2).
Rnd 14: [RTW, p2, LTW, p2] 10 times.
Rnd 15: [(P1, k1, p1) twice, p2] 10 times.
Rnd 16: [P1, RTW, LTW, p3] 10 times.
Rnd 17: [P2, k2, p4] 10 times.
Rnd 18: [P2, LTW, p4] 10 times.
Rnds 19–21: [P2, k2, p4] 10 times.
Rnd 22: [P2, LTW, p4] 10 times.
Rnds 23–25: [P2, k2, p4] 10 times.
Rnd 26: [P2, LTW, p4] 10 times.

Rnd 27: [P2, k2, p4] 10 times.
Rnd 28: [P1, LTW, RTW, p3] 10 times.
Rnd 29: [(P1, k1, p1) twice, p2] 10 times.
Rnd 30: [LTW, p2, RTW, p2] 10 times.
Rnd 31: [K1, p4, k1, p2] 10 times.
Begin rnd 32 on peg 80. The LTW will straddle the two rounds/rows.
Rnd 32: *LTW, p4, RTW, rep from * to last stitch, skip 1 wyib.
Rnds 33–64: Rep rnds 1–32 (1 time).
Rnds 65–71: Rep rnds 1–7 (1 time). Length may be adjusted to suit by working more rnds.
Bind off using the gather method.

Finishing

Weave in ends and block lightly.

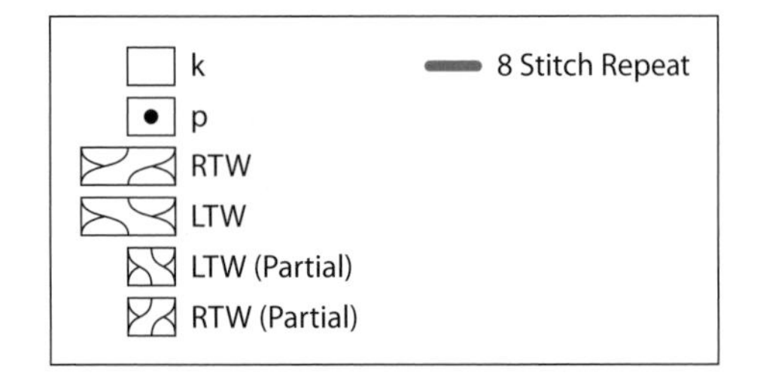

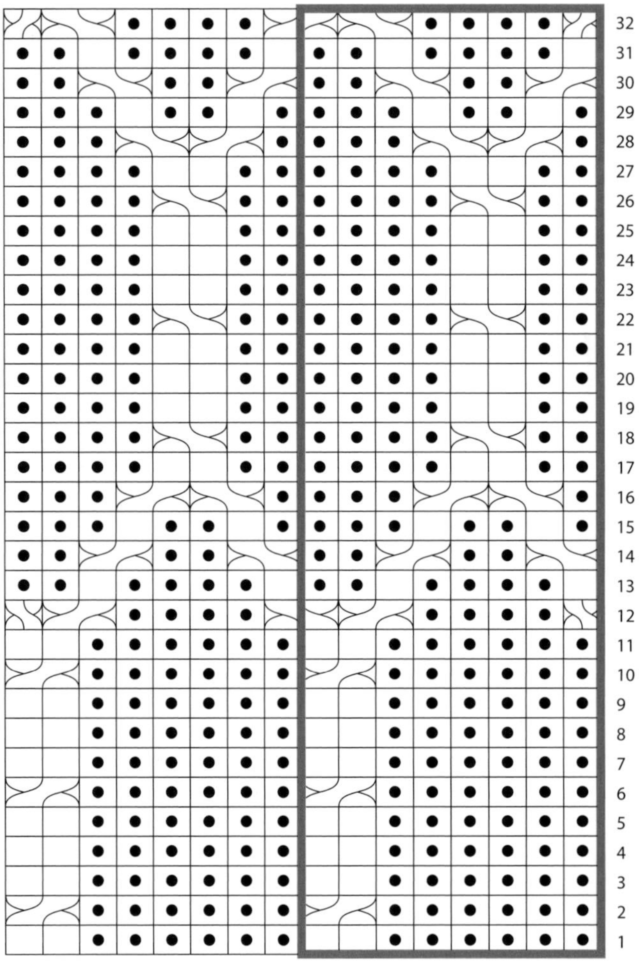

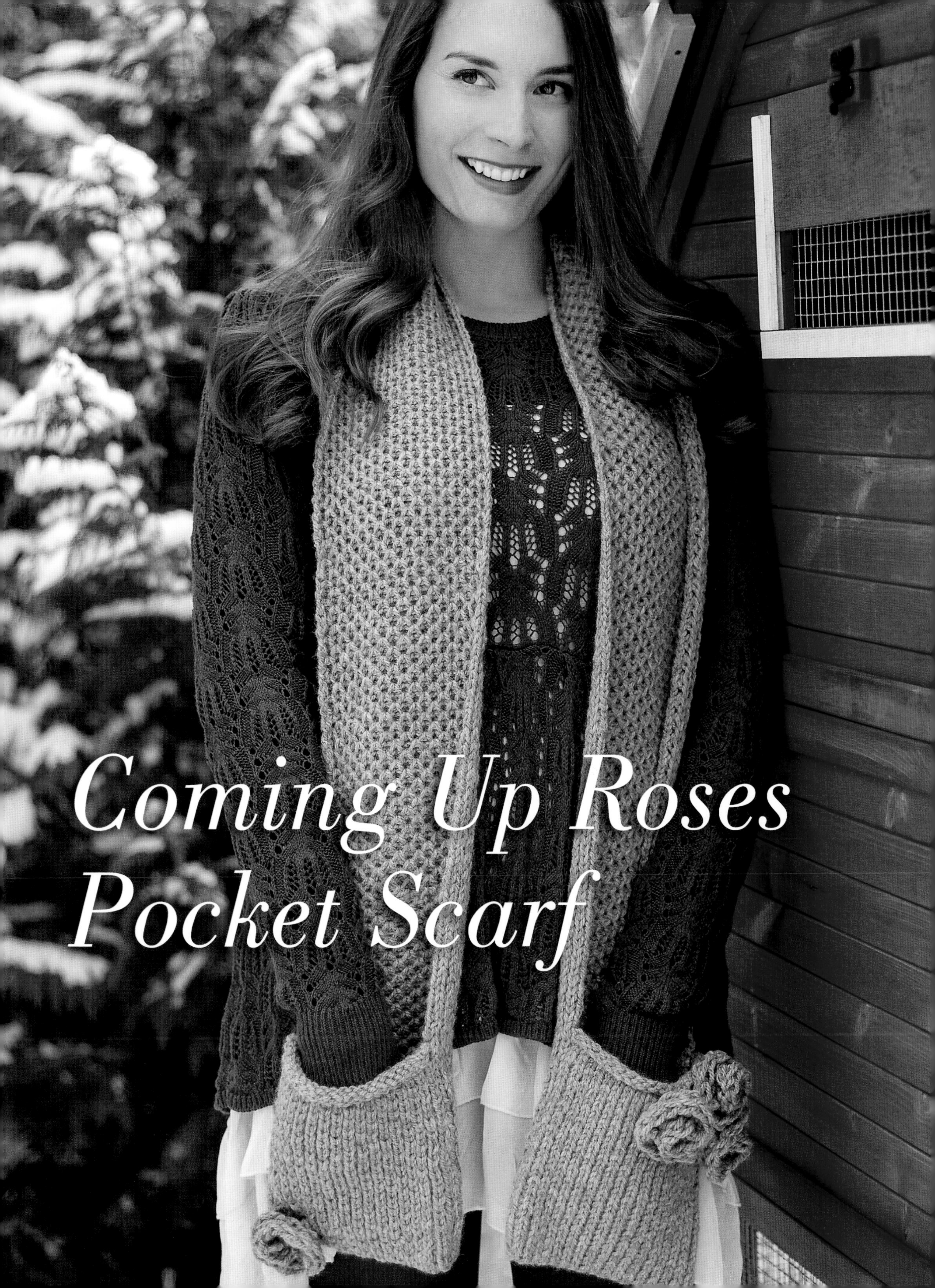

Coming Up Roses Pocket Scarf

A handsome, reversible tuck stitch gives beautiful texture to this scarf. The ends of the scarf are turned up and seamed, creating pockets to keep those hands warm on the coldest of days. Roses are then added to complete the look.

Level

Beginner

Finished Measurements

8 in/20.3 cm wide x 73 in/185.4 cm long after pockets are turned up and seamed

Gauge

12 sts and 18 rows = 4 in/10.2 cm in tuck stitch

Yarn

Plymouth Yarn Encore Chunky, bulky weight #5 (75% acrylic, 25% wool; 143 yd/131 m, 3.5 oz/100 g per skein) 3 skeins #0678 Green Gray

Supplies

- 11⁄16 in/1.75 cm peg spacing loom with at least 24 pegs
- Knitting tool
- Crochet hook
- Measuring tape
- Yarn/tapestry needle
- Cable needle (optional)

Special Stitches

Tuck knit: On rows where there are multiple sts on the pegs (created by the skipped sts with yarn in front of peg) and you are instructed to knit, use the regular knit stitch to knit all sts together, creating the tuck.

MB (make bobble): Make an e-wrap knit stitch by making an e-wrap and lifting the bottom loop over the top wrap (you may wish to keep this stitch on a cable needle for easier lifting later). Make 4 more e-wrap knit stitches on the same peg. Reach down below the peg and pick up the first e-wrap knit stitch and lift it onto the peg. E-wrap knit all stitches on peg together as one.

Pattern Notes

- If substituting yarn, use a natural fiber blend or 100 percent natural fiber, as this scarf requires blocking to lie flat. Alternatively, you may add sts for a garter or ribbed edge.
- Make the 4 roses first to ensure that you have enough yarn.
- For photo-illustrated instructions on how to make a bobble (MB), see pages 119–20.

Scarf

Begin top edge of pocket.

Foundation row: Chain CO 24 sts.

Rows 1–4: Knit.

Begin pattern stitch.

Row 1: Skip1 wyib, *k1, skip1 wyif, rep from * to last 2 sts, k2.

Row 2: Skip1 wyib, k1, *skip1 wyif, rep from * to last 2 sts, k2.

Row 3: Skip1 wyib, knit to end of row (tuck knit the pegs with multiple sts on them).
Rows 4–5: K1, *skip1 wyif, k1, rep from * to end of row.
Row 6: As row 3.
Rep rows 1–6 until scarf measures 89 in/226 cm. You may adjust this measurement by measuring recipient from fingertip to fingertip, taking tape around neck and then adding 16 in/40.6 cm for the pockets.
Next 4 rows: Knit.
Chain one bind-off.

Finishing

Weave in all ends. Fold edges of scarf up 8 in/20.3 cm and seam sides using mattress stitch.

Bobble Roses (make 4)

Foundation row: Chain CO 24 sts.
Row 1: K1, purl to last st, k1.
Row 2: K2, yo-k2tog, *MB, k1, yo-k2tog, rep from * to end.
Row 3: As row 1.
Row 4: K2tog, knit to last 2 sts, ssk. (22 sts)
Row 5: *K1, yo-k2tog, rep from * to last st, k1.
Row 6: K1, p2tog, purl to last 3 sts, ssp, k1. (20 sts)
Row 7: K2tog, knit to last 2 sts, ssk. (18 sts)
Bind off using gather method, leaving a long tail.
Pull the tail to gather, overlapping the bind-off edge, and secure. Use tail to sew the roses to the scarf. Refer to the picture for placement.

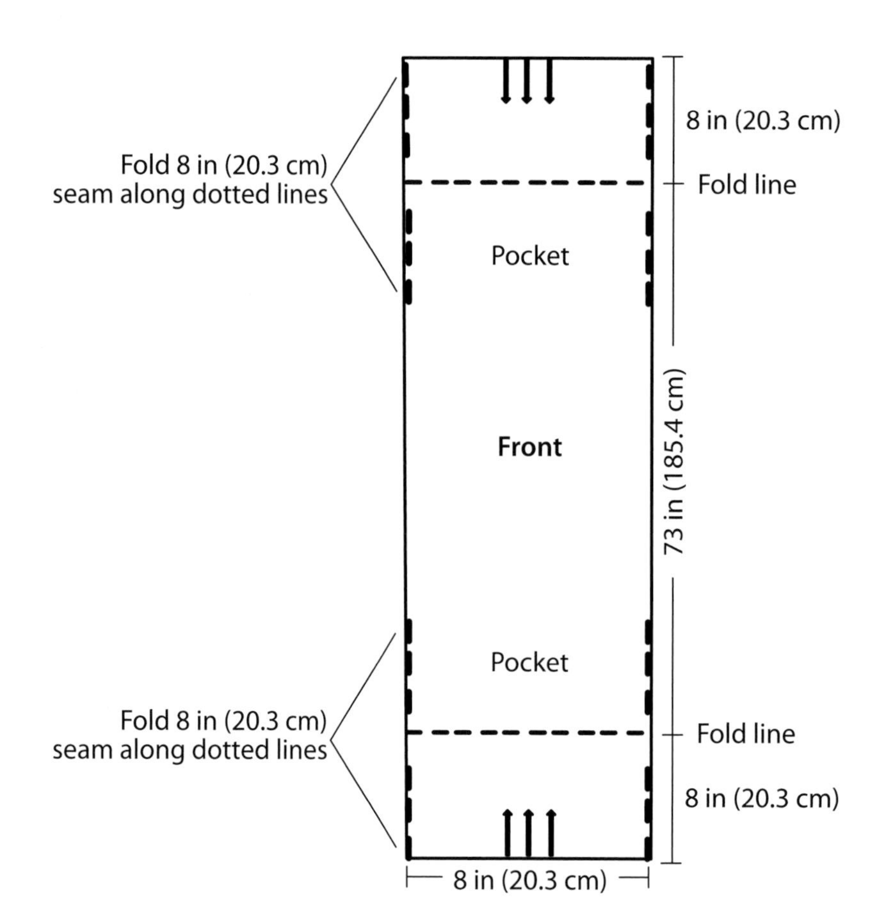

Sleuthhound Visor Cap

This sporty, traditional hat is part deerstalker (think Sherlock) and part baseball cap. A shaped crown makes for a nice fit and handsome profile.

Level

Confident Beginner

Finished Measurements

Adult: Approximately 8 in/20.3 cm tall x 20 in/50.8 cm circumference

Large child/small teen: 7 in/17.8 cm tall x 18 in/45.7 cm circumference

Instructions are written for size adult, with child/teen size instructions in parentheses. If only one instruction is given, it applies to both sizes.

Gauge

16 sts and 36 rows = 4 in/10.2 cm in stockinette stitch

Yarn

Lion Brand Vanna's Choice, worsted weight #4 (100% acrylic; 170 yd/155 m, 3.5 oz/100 g per skein)
1 skein #125 Taupe (MC)

Stitch Studio by Nicole Studio Basic, worsted weight #4 (100% acrylic; 170 yd/155 m, 3.5 oz/100 g per skein)
1 skein #240479-5 Wine (CC)

Supplies

- ⅜ in/1 cm peg spacing round loom with 80 pegs (adult) or 72 pegs (child/teen)
- Knitting tool
- Measuring tape
- Crochet hook
- 2 stitch markers
- Yarn/tapestry needle

Pattern Notes

- Hat is knit from the bottom up, beginning with the visor.
- The visor is knit flat and then the main body of the hat is knit in the round.
- The top of the hat is decreased in four equal wedges and then seamed closed.
- When asked to CO1, use the true cable cast-on method as described on page 110.

Pattern

VISOR

Foundation row: Chain CO 15 (11) pegs with 1 strand MC; work as flat panel.
Row 1: Skip1, knit to end.
Row 2: Skip1, purl to end.
Row 3: CO1, knit to end, CO1.
Row 4: Skip1, purl to end. (17 sts)
Rows 5–20: Rep rows 3 and 4 (8 times). (33 sts)
Chain CO all remaining pegs and join to work in the round. Place a stitch marker on the peg with the join; this will be your new peg 1 (beginning of your round).

BODY OF HAT

Rnds 1 and 3: Knit.
Rnds 2 and 4: Purl.
Cut MC and change to CC.
Row 5: Knit.
Row 6: Purl.
Rows 7–14: Rep rows 5 and 6 (4 times).
Row 15: Knit.
Cut CC and change to MC.
Row 16: Knit.
Rep row 16 until body of hat measures 5½ in/13.3 cm (4¾ in/12.1 cm), not including visor. You may adjust this measurement to fit recipient's head.

TOP OF HAT DECREASES

You will be working in 4 sections of 20 (18) stitches each, making 4 wedges that gradually decrease from 20 (18) stitches to 2 stitches. You will seam these sections together when the hat is complete. Work your first section centered over the brim. Find the center of your brim and place a marker 10 (9) sts to either side of center. You will need to cut your working yarn to do this.

Wedge

Row 1: Knit.
Row 2: K2tog, knit to last 2 sts, ssk.
Rep rows 1 and 2 until there are 2 stitches left.
Chain one bind-off, leaving a long tail for seaming.

Rep Wedge instructions over the next 20 (18) stitches 3 more times. There will be a total of 4 wedges.

Using mattress stitch, close to the edges, seam the wedges and close the top of the hat. Weave in ends.

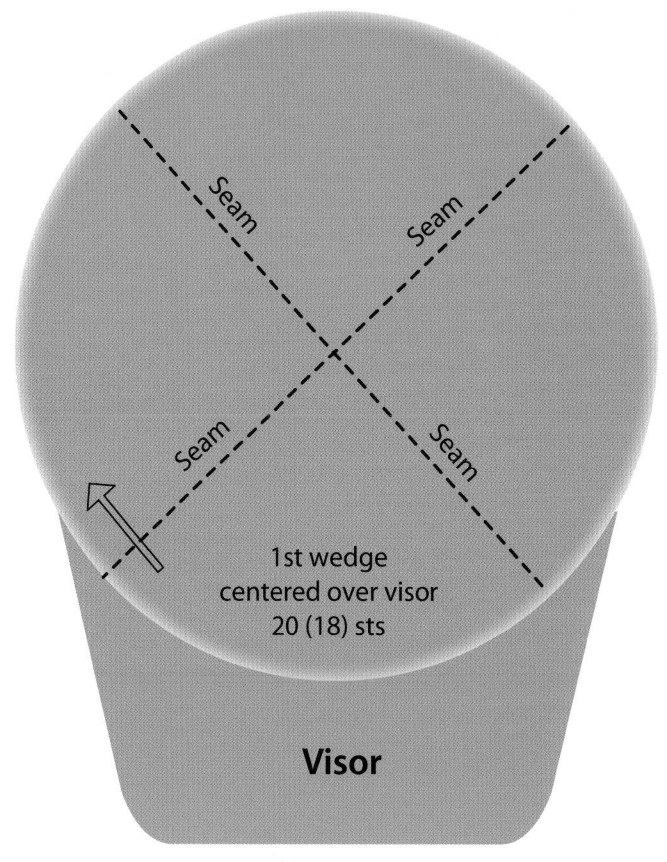

Hat is viewed from top down

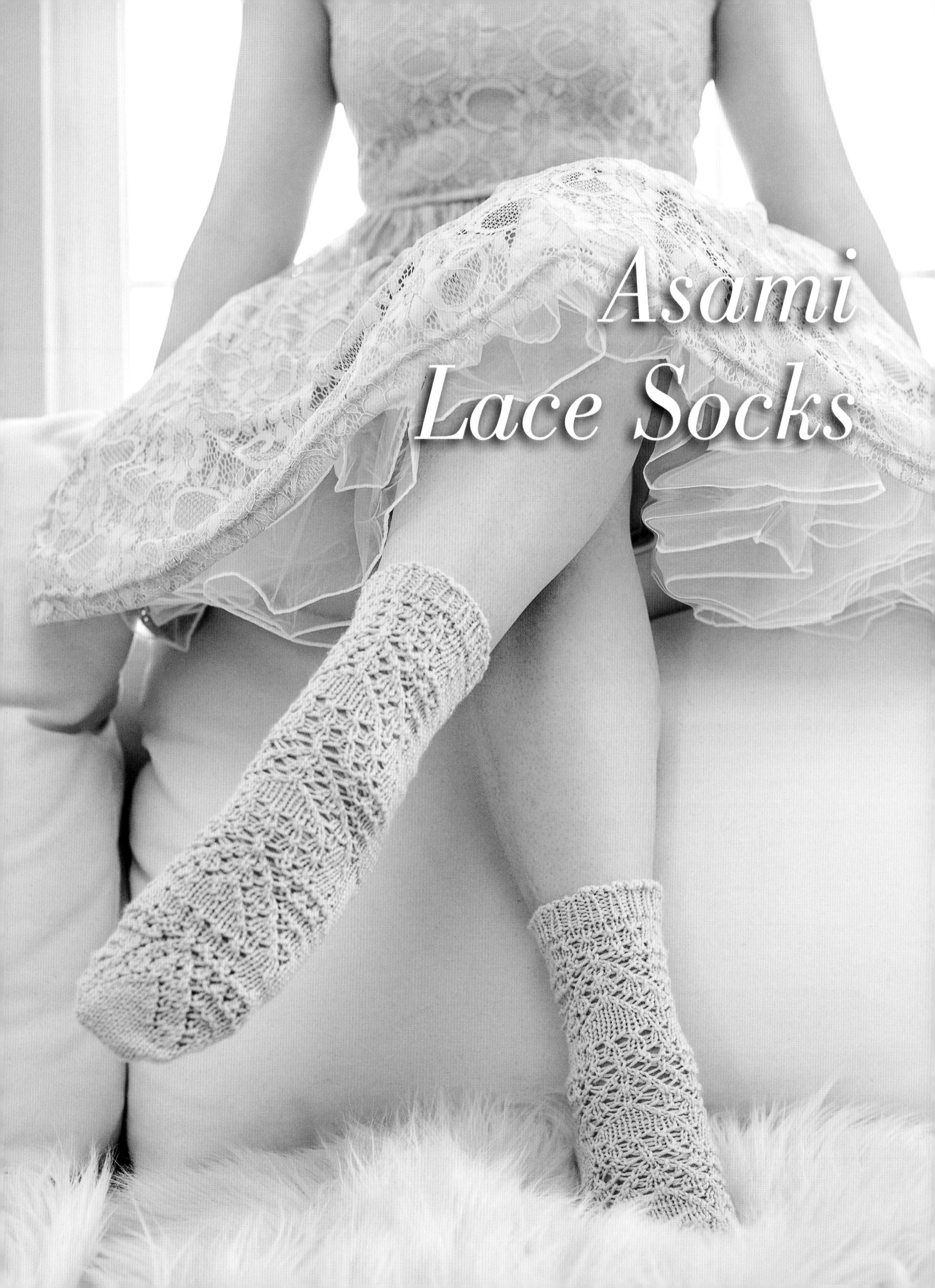

Asami Lace Socks

Asami means "morning beauty" in Japanese—a fitting name for these luxurious boot socks. I'm very intrigued by Japanese lace knitting, and these short boot socks showcase it wonderfully. They are thicker than regular socks, worked from the toe up using sport weight, superwash wool and the Kitchener cast-on.

Level

Advanced

Finished Measurements/Size

14 in/35.6 cm long x 8.5 in/21.6 cm circumference (length is adjustable)

To fit adult ladies, medium width.

Gauge

19 sts and 36 rows = 4 in/10.2 cm in lace stitch

22 sts and 36 rows = 4 in/10.2 cm in stockinette stitch

Yarn

Cascade Yarns 220 Superwash, sport weight #3 (100% superwash wool; 137 yd/125 m, 1.8 oz/51 g per skein)

1 skein #1941 Salmon

Supplies

- 3/8 in/1 cm peg spacing round loom with 40 pegs
- Knitting tool
- Measuring tape
- Crochet hook
- 3 stitch markers
- Yarn/tapestry needle

Special Abbreviations

cf: Count forward

mf: Move forward

mb: Move back

Pattern Notes

- Socks are knit from the toe up.
- Toe and heel must be worked on opposite sides of the loom.
- Lace pattern is worked on the toe side of the loom.
- ***Important:*** During the lace portion of the sock, you will occasionally have multiple sts on one peg; always knit those sts together as you come to them. This step will not be noted within the pattern itself.

- Place markers on pegs 20, 22, and 38 (40-peg loom).
- A chain two bind-off is used to encourage extra stretch and give a "frilly" appearance to the top of the sock.
- Sample sock used 4 repeats of lace pattern.
- For photo-illustrated instructions on Kitchener cast-on, u-knit stitch, wrap and turn (w&t), counting forward (cf), moving forward (mf), and moving back (mb), see pages 110–11, 114, 117, 123, and 124.

Pattern

TOE/HEEL

Kitchener CO all 40 pegs.

Foundation round: K40 (use regular knit stitch to lock in cast-on).

Decrease Toe (worked flat)

Begin decreasing toe, working over 20 pegs using short rows; use u-knit from now on.

Row 1: U-k19, w&t next peg.
Row 2: U-k18, w&t next peg.
Row 3: U-k17, w&t next peg.
Row 4: U-k16, w&t next peg.
Row 5: U-k15, w&t next peg.
Row 6: U-k14, w&t next peg.
Row 7: U-k13, w&t next peg.
Row 8: U-k12, w&t next peg.
Row 9: U-k11, w&t next peg.
Row 10: U-k10, w&t next peg (5 wraps on either side of toe/heel).

Begin increasing toe, working wraps as you come to them.

Row 11: U-k to the 1st wrapped peg, pick up wraps by knitting sts together, turn.
Row 12: Rep row 11, do not u-k the 1st st in the row (or last st knit in row 11).

Rep rows 11 and 12 until you've picked up the last wrapped peg on both sides of the toe, w&t the next peg.

Last row of increase: Knit to end of row.

FOOT (WORK IN THE ROUND)

Take Measurement A: Measure your foot from toe to where your heel begins. Alternatively, measure the length of your whole foot and subtract 1½ to 2 in/3.8 to 5.1 cm.

Rnds 1 and 2: U-k40, working any leftover wraps as you do rnd 1.

Lace

Rnd 1: K21, psso, k1, yo-k2tog, k5, ssk-yo, k1, psso, k2.
Rnd 2: Knit.
Rnd 3: K21, p1, yo-k2tog, k2, yo-k2tog, k1, [k2, ssk-yo] twice, p1, k2.
Rnd 4: Knit.
Rnd 5: K23, psso, k1, yo-k2tog, k1, ssk-yo, k1, psso, k4.
Rnd 6: Knit.
Rnd 7: K21, P3, yo-k2tog, k2, psso, k2, ssk-yo, p3, k2.
Rnd 8: Knit.
Rnd 9: K22, [k3, psso] twice, k6.
Rnd 10: Knit.
Rnd 11: K21, p5, yo-k2tog, psso, ssk-yo, p5, k2.
Rnd 12: Knit.
Rnd 13: K21, yo-k2tog 4 times, k1, ssk-yo 4 times, k2.
Rnd 14: Knit.
Rnd 15: K21, p7, psso, p7, k2.
Rnd 16: Knit.
Rnd 17: K21, cf2-mb1, cf3-mb1, cf4-mb1, k3, yo, k1, [yo-k2tog] 4 times, cf3-mf1, cf2-mf1, cf1-mf1, yo, k5.

Rnds 18–20: Knit.

Rnds 21–28: Rep rnds 17–20 (twice).

Rep rnds 1–28 of lace until your sock equals Measurement A. Do not include bottom of toe in this measurement. You may wish to close your sock at this point (see Kitchener Cast-on on pages 110–11 for further instructions) to get the most accurate measurement of the knitting. Keep track of the rnd you stopped working on; you will begin with the next row after completing the heel. ***Example:*** If you stopped on rnd 10, then begin knitting on rnd 11 after the heel is complete.

Heel

Begin heel on opposite side of where you worked the toe, over 20 pegs using short rows, repeating the directions above for the toe beginning on row 1 (stop working in the round).

Resume Lace

Begin working the lace pattern where you left off until the top portion of your sock measures 7 in/17.8 cm (you may adjust this measurement to suit, adding/subtracting lace repeats). You will be working in the round once again.

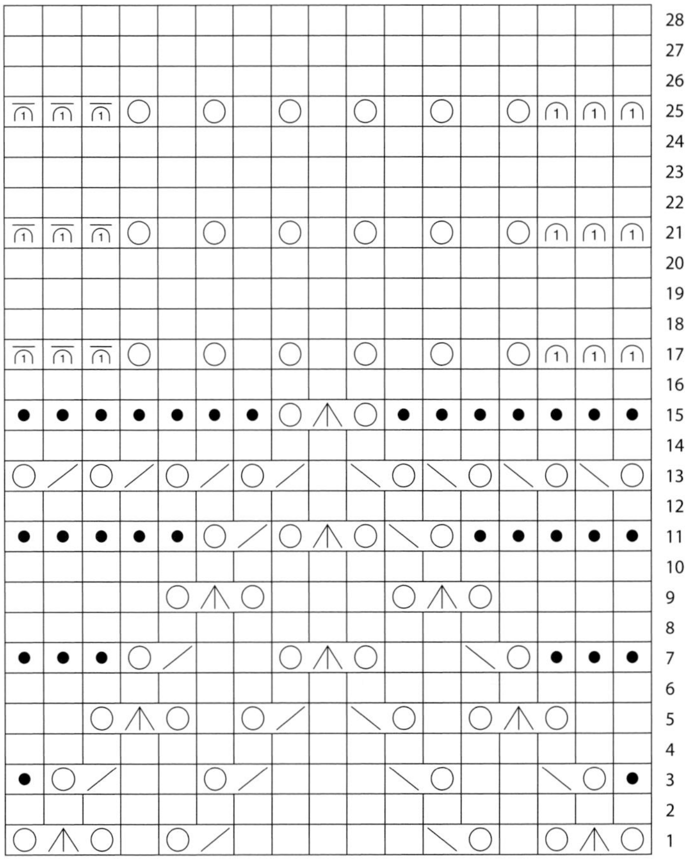

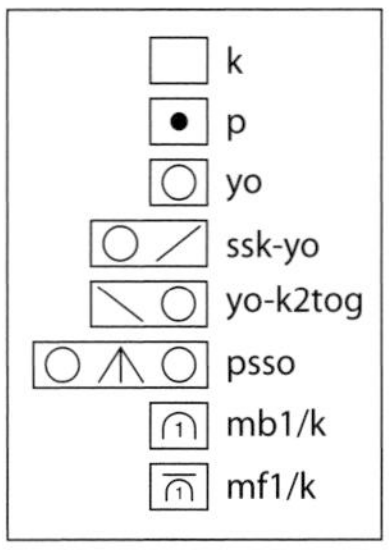

RIBBING

Rnds 1–7: *U-k1, p1, rep from * to end of round.

Chain two bind-off all sts.

Finishing

Close toe of sock and weave in ends.

LACE SECTION

k
p
yo
ssk-yo
yo-k2tog
psso
mb1/k
mf1/k

Tips for Using Other Looms/Sizes

HEEL AND TOE must be decreased by half. Divide the total number of pegs in half, then divide that number in half again, and you will get the number you must decrease (this should be the number of wraps on the loom before increasing again).

Work the heel and toe on opposite sides of the loom, just like the pattern.

The lace portion is worked over 17 sts; center the 17 sts on the toe side of the loom and use stitch markers to guide you. Add/subtract the number of u-knit stitches necessary on either side of the lace markers. You always u-knit up to and beyond the markers.

Reference the chart for stitch placement.

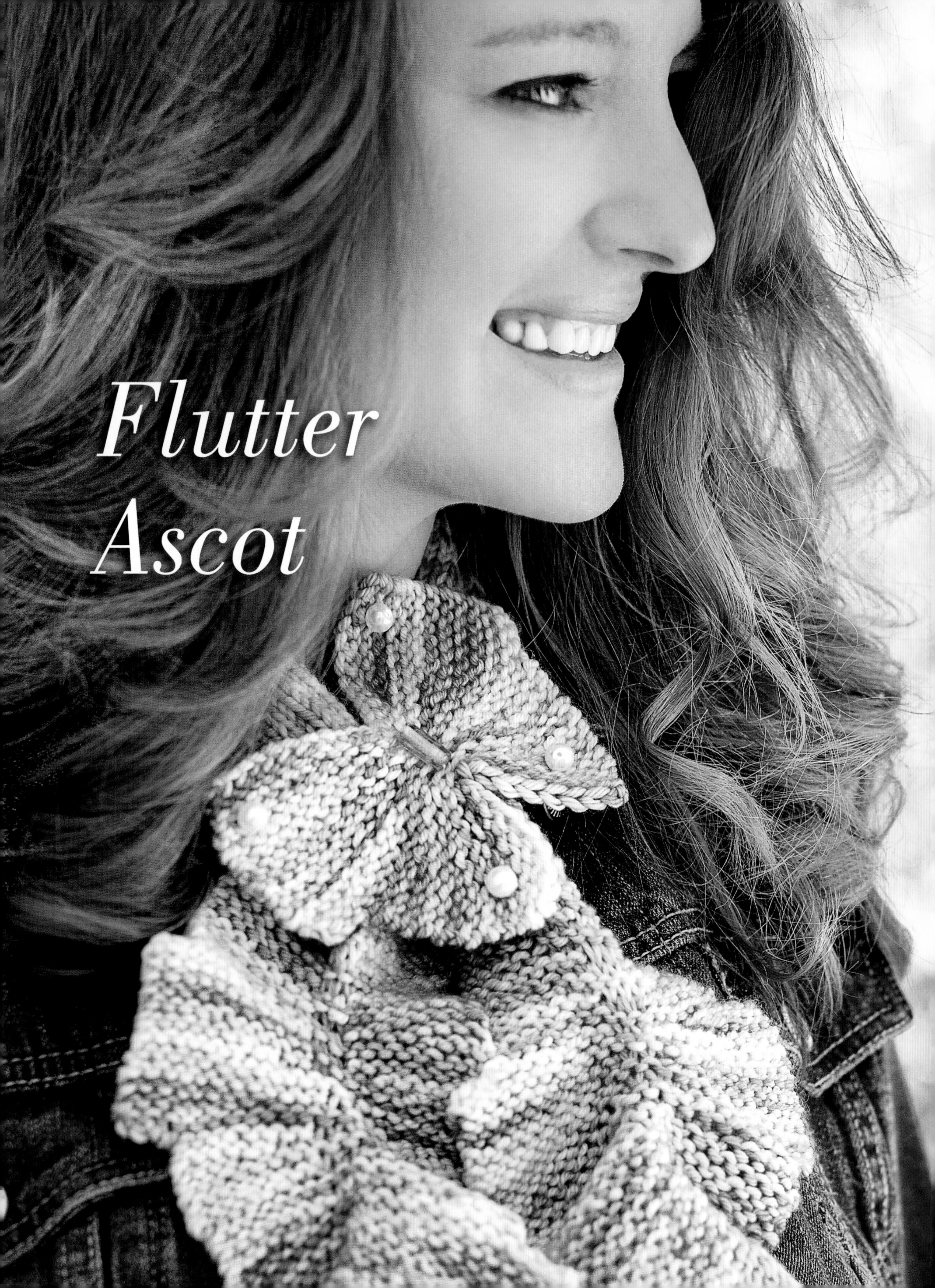

Flutter Ascot

A series of whimsical butterflies worked with garter stitch, short rows, and hand-dyed yarn creates an easy springtime, ruffled scarflet. A separate butterfly tie acts as an accent piece at the neck area.

Level

Confident Beginner

Finished Measurements

4½ in/11.4 cm wide x 33 in/83.8 cm long after blocking

Gauge

16 sts and 30 rows = 4 in/10.2 cm square in garter stitch
22 sts and 22 rows = 4 in/10.2 cm square in stockinette stitch

Yarn

June Pryce Fiber Arts Greenwich Worsted, worsted weight #4 (100% superwash merino wool; 218 yd/199.3 m, 3.5 oz/100 g per skein)
1 skein Up a Creek

Supplies

- ⅜ in/1 cm peg spacing loom with at least 24 pegs
- Knitting tool
- Crochet hook
- Measuring tape
- Yarn/tapestry needle
- 4 large pearl beads
- 1 oblong 1.5 in/3.8 cm bead

Pattern Notes

- Main scarf is worked first, and then a separate butterfly tie is made.
- The main scarf is knit as one piece. A series of butterflies, using short rows, are worked on each end of the scarf, creating a ruffled look.
- The ribbed neck section may be shortened or lengthened to accommodate different sizes.
- The yarn used is hand-dyed, and colors may vary.

Main Scarf

SIDE A: FIRST HALF OF BUTTERFLY

Foundation row: Chain CO 18 pegs; work as flat panel.
Row 1: K8, turn.
Row 2: P8, turn.
Row 3: K6, turn.
Row 4: P6, turn.
Row 5: K4, turn.
Row 6: P4, turn.
Row 7: K18.
Row 8: P8, turn.
Row 9: K8, turn.
Row 10: P6, turn.
Row 11: K6, turn.
Row 12: P4, turn.
Row 13: K4, turn.
Row 14: P18.
Rows 15–42: Rep rows 1–14 (2 times), making wedges on each side of the scarf.

SIDE B: SECOND HALF OF BUTTERFLY

Row 43: CO3, K11, turn.
Row 44: P11, turn.
Row 45: K9, turn.
Row 46: P9, turn.
Row 47: K7, turn.
Row 48: P7, turn.

Row 49: K21, CO3.
Row 50: P11, turn.
Row 51: K11, turn.
Row 52: P9, turn.
Row 53: K9, turn.
Row 54: P7, turn.
Row 55: K7, turn.
Row 56: P24.
Rows 57–70: Rep rows 43–56 (1 time), ignoring the cast-on instructions on rows 43 and 49.
Row 71–83: Rep rows 43–55 (1 time), ignoring the cast-on instructions on rows 43 and 49.
Row 84: BO3, p21.
Rep rows 1–84, binding off 3 stitches at the beginning of row 1 (1 time), 2 more times. There will be 18 sts on Side A and 24 sts for Side B.

RIBBED NECK SECTION

Row 1: [K2, p1] 3 times, k6, [p1, k2] 3 times.
Rep row 1 until total work measures 24 in/61 cm or desired length.

SECOND END OF SCARF

Begin on Side B, ignoring the cast-on instructions as you already have 24 sts on the loom. Work Side B, then Side A (3 times). Scarf will end on Side A. Chain one bind-off when work is complete.

Butterfly Tie

Work Side A and then Side B once of butterfly (ending on row 90); chain one bind-off after Side B is complete.

2-STITCH I-CORD CLOSURE

Chain CO 2 sts.
Row 1: Knit peg 2, knit peg 1.
Rep row 1 until cord measures 4½ in/11.4 cm.

Finishing

Weave in ends. Block the scarf. Sew butterfly tie to center of I-cord closure. Loop the I-cord around both sides of scarf just above the ruffled area and sew ends of I-cord together. The I-cord closure should freely slide up and down scarf to tighten at the neck when wearing. To finish butterfly, add 1 pearl bead to each corner of butterfly and 1 oblong bead to the center.

Overlapping Waves Mitts

Hand-dyed yarn and lace stitches come together to make an elegant mitt pattern. A grafted thumb gusset creates a comfortable mitt. This is a lovely, lightweight, sophisticated mitt when completed.

Level

Advanced

Finished Measurements

9 in/22.9 cm long x 9 in/22.9 cm circumference

Instructions are given in pattern for adjustments to fit larger or smaller hands.

Gauge

20 sts and 32 rows = 4 in/10.2 cm square in overlapping waves stitch

Yarn

Miss Babs Yowza! Whatta Skein!, light worsted weight #3 (100% merino wool; 560 yd/512 m, 8 oz/227 g per skein) 1 skein or less Wild Iris

Supplies

- 3/8 in/1 cm peg spacing loom with at least 36 pegs
- Knitting tool
- Crochet hook
- Measuring tape
- Stitch markers
- Yarn/tapestry needle

Special Stitches

1x1 ribbing: Single knit stitches alternate with single purl stitches, creating very narrow columns. To create 1x1 ribbing, work every row: *K1, p1; rep from * to end of row. On the second row, knit the knits and purl the purls. Keep track by using stitch markers to mark your knits or purls just at the beginning of the row, as the increases/decreases may throw you off.

k2tog: Knit two stitches together. In this pattern the k2tog is worked differently on the lace rows (rows with cf's/

mb's, as row 3) than the normal k2tog, as the stitches will already have been moved. There is no need for further movement of the stitches on these rows. On rows such as row 1, you will do a regular k2tog, where you move your sts as normal (see page 120).

Special Abbreviations

cf: Count forward
mf: Move forward

Pattern Notes

- This yarn is hand-dyed, so color will vary. The lighter the colorway you choose, the more the pattern will stand out. Yarn weight is closer to DK than worsted.
- Mitts are worked flat in 2 sections, main mitt and thumb, and then seamed together.
- For photo-illustrated instructions on how to count forward (cf) and move forward (mf), see pages 123–24.
- When asked to CO1, use the true cable cast-on method as described on page 110.

Mitt Body

RIBBING

Size Teen/Small only:
Foundation row: Chain CO 36 sts; work as flat panel.
Rows 1–2: Work in 1x1 ribbing.
Row 3: CO 1 stitch, 1x1 rib stitch to end of row, CO 1 stitch. (38 sts)
Rows 4–6: Rep rows 1–3 (1 time). (40 sts)
Rows 7–8: Work in 1x1 ribbing.

Size Medium/Large only:
Foundation row: Chain CO 40 sts; work as flat panel.
Rows 1–8: Work in 1x1 ribbing.

PATTERN STITCH (ALL SIZES)

Row 1: K2, *yo-k2tog, k4, rep from * to last 2 sts, k2.
Row 2: Knit.
Row 3: K2, *cf2-mf1, cf1-mf1, yo, k1, k2tog, k3, rep from * to last 2 sts, k2.
Row 4: Knit.
Row 5: K2, *cf3-mf1, cf2-mf1, cf1-mf1, yo, k2, k2tog, k2, rep form * to last 2 sts, k2.
Row 6: Knit.
Row 7: K2, *cf4-mf1, cf3-mf1, cf2-mf1, cf1-mf1, yo, k3, k2tog, k1, rep from * to last 2 sts, k2.

Row 8: Knit.
Row 9: K2, *cf5-mf1, cf4-mf1, cf3-mf1, cf2-mf1, cf1-mf1, yo, k4, k2tog, rep from * to last 2 sts, k2.
Row 10: Knit.
Rows 11–60: Rep rows 1–10 (5 times) or until total knitting measures 8 in/20.3 cm.

RIBBING

Size Teen/Small only:
Rows 1–2: Work in 1x1 ribbing.
Row 3: K2tog, 1x1 rib stitch to end of row, ssk. (38 sts)
Rows 4–6: Rep rows 1–3 (1 time). (36 sts)
Rows 7–8: Work in 1x1 ribbing.
Chain one bind-off all sts.

Size Medium/Large only:
Rows 1–8: Work in 1x1 ribbing.
Chain one bind-off all sts.

Thumb Gusset

Foundation row: Chain CO 16 (18) pegs.
Row 1: *K1, p1, rep to last 2 sts, k2.
Row 2: K1, *k1, p1, rep to last st, k1.
Row 3: As row 1.
Row 4: As row 2.
Row 5–14: Knit.
Row 15: K2tog, knit to last 2 sts, ssk.
Row 16: Knit.
Rows 17–20: Rep rows 15 and 16 (2 times).
Row 21: K2tog, knit to last 2 pegs, ssk.
Rep row 21 until there are 4 sts left on the loom.
Next row: K2tog, ssk.
Next row: K2tog.
Bind off, leaving a long tail for seaming.
Seam top of gusset: Fold gusset in half. Seam from top of gusset (rib end) to where gusset starts to decrease. Stop seaming; continue to Finishing.

Finishing

Read all directions before starting: Fold mitt in half RS out. *Seam from top of mitt 2¼ to 2½ in/5.7 to 6.4 cm; do not weave in tail. Seam from bottom of mitt (wrist/arm end) 4½ in/11.4 cm; do not weave in tail (indicated in green). Place your hand inside mitt* and line up thumb gusset and mitt. Seam bottom sides of thumb gusset to sides of mitt (indicated in red), making sure the tube remains open for your thumb. Finish sewing the side seams to meet thumb gusset (indicated in blue). Weave in ends. For second mitt, flip it upside down so that waves are going in the opposite direction before seaming as above. ***Note:*** If you do not want a thumb gusset, follow above directions from * to * and then use a pin to mark where your thumb stops and starts, and seam to those pins. Try on mitt before weaving in the ends, to ensure proper fit.

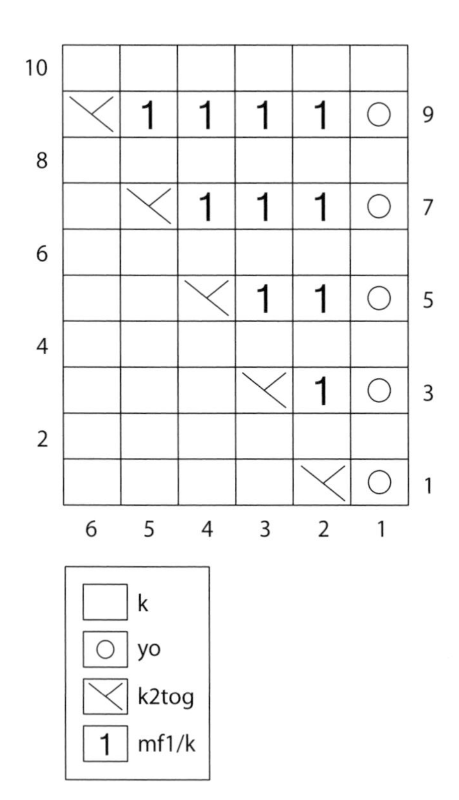

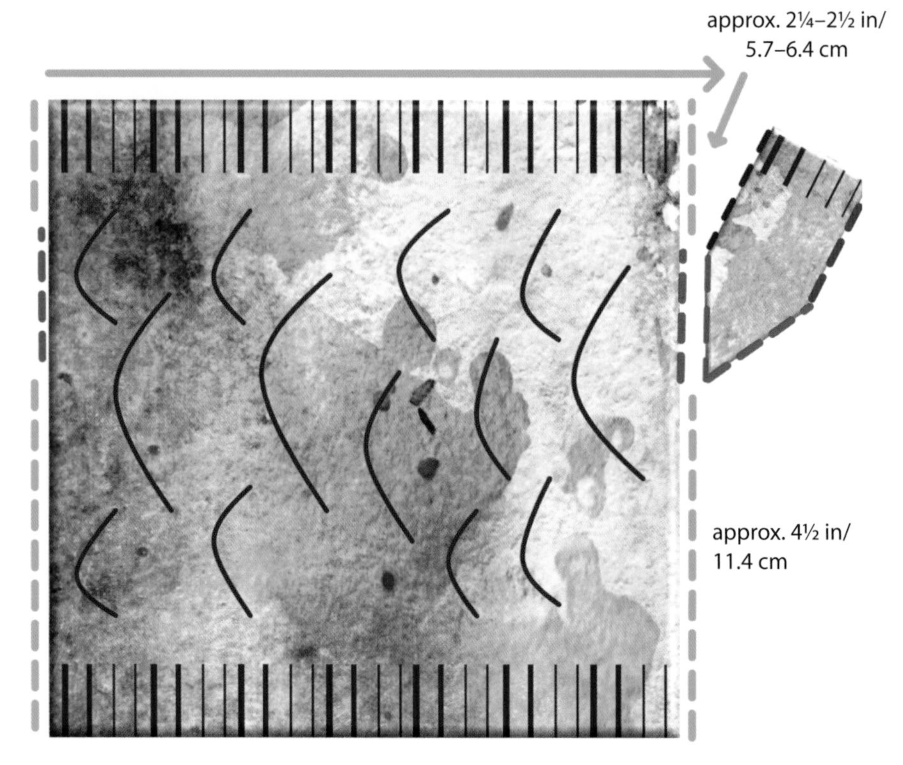

Adrift Cowl

A random floating pattern like an abstract painting is created by using short rows on this unusual cowl. Although it looks complicated, it isn't, only requiring garter stitch and randomly changing directions. Before you know it, you'll have a work of art that's wearable!

Level

Confident Beginner

Finished Measurements

10 in/25.4 cm high x 20 in/50.8 cm circumference after blocking

Gauge

20 sts and 32 rows = 4 in/10.2 cm square in garter stitch

Yarn

Three Irish Girls Yarn Springvale DK, light weight #3 (100% superwash merino; 270 yd/246.8 m; 3.5 oz/100 g per skein)
1 skein #56590 Jolene Quiet (MC)
The Periwinkle Sheep Merino DK, light weight #3 (100% superwash merino; 225 yd/205.7 m, 3.5 oz/100 g per skein)
1 skein #56139 Copper Pipe (CC)

Supplies

- 3/8 in/1 cm peg spacing round loom with 88 pegs
- Knitting tool
- Stitch markers
- Measuring tape

Pattern Notes

- Caution! Acrylics/synthetics are not recommended for this pattern, as it requires blocking to lie flat due to the short rows. Please use wool or another natural fiber.
- Place marker every 8th peg before beginning. This will help guide you during the short rows.
- When a leaf (ML) is called for, stop working in the round and begin short rows, changing direction after every wrap and turn. Work wrapped pegs as you come to them.
- When a leaf overlaps the next round, work leftover wraps on the following round.
- Occasional interruptions in the garter stitch pattern are to be expected.
- For photo-illustrated instructions on how to work the wrap and turn short rows (w&t), see page 117.

Stitch Patterns

ML-1 (Make Leaf 1)

Row 1: K7, w&t.
Row 2: P6, w&t.
Row 3: K5, w&t.
Row 4: P4, w&t.
Row 5: K3, w&t.
Row 6: P2, w&t.
Row 7: K1, w&t.
Row 8: P4, w&t.
Row 9: K16.

ML-2 (Make Leaf 2)

Row 1: K16, w&t.
Row 2: P15, w&t.
Row 3: K14, w&t.
Row 4: P13, w&t.
Row 5: K12, w&t.
Row 6: P11, w&t.
Row 7: K10, w&t.
Row 8: P9, w&t.
Row 9: K8, w&t.
Row 10: P7, w&t.
Row 11: K6, w&t.
Row 12: P5, w&t.
Row 13: K4, w&t.
Row 14: P3, w&t.
Row 15: K4, w&t.
Row 16: P5, w&t.
Row 17: K6, w&t.
Row 18: P7, w&t.
Row 19: K8, w&t.
Row 20: P13, w&t.
Row 21: K24. (K16 on last leaf.)

ML-3 (Make Leaf 3)

Row 1: K8, w&t.
Row 2: P7, w&t.
Row 3: K6, w&t.
Row 4: P5, w&t.
Row 5: K4, w&t.
Row 6: P3, w&t.
Row 7: K2, w&t.
Row 8: P5, w&t.
Row 9: K9, w&t.
Row 10: P8, w&t.
Row 11: K7, w&t.
Row 12: P6, w&t.
Row 13: K5, w&t.
Row 14: P4, w&t.
Row 15: K3, w&t.
Row 16: P2, w&t.
Row 17: K12. (On the last leaf, knit to end of round.)

Pattern

Foundation round: Chain CO all pegs with 1 strand MC; join to work in the round.
Rnd 1 (in MC): Purl.
Rnd 2 (in MC): Knit.
Rnd 3 (in MC): Purl.
Rnd 4 (in MC): *ML-1, rep from * to last 8 sts, ML-1, k8.
Rnd 5 (in CC): Knit.
Rnd 6 (in CC): Purl.
Rnd 7 (in MC): Knit.
Rnd 8 (in MC): Purl.
Rnd 9 (in CC): K8, *ML-1, rep from * to end.
Rnd 10 (in CC): Purl.
Rnd 11 (in MC): Knit.
Rnd 12 (in MC): Purl.
Rnds 13–14 (in MC): Rep rnds 11–12 (1 time).
Rnd 15 (in CC): Knit.
Rnd 16 (in CC): Purl.
Rnd 17 (in MC): *ML-2, rep from * to end of round.
Rnd 18 (in MC): Purl.
Rnd 19 (in CC): Knit.
Rnd 20 (in CC): Purl.
Rnds 21–22 (in CC): Rep rnds 19–20 (1 time).
Rnd 23 (in MC): Knit.
Rnd 24 (in MC): Purl.
Rnd 25 (in CC): *ML-3, rep from * to end of round (on row 17 of last leaf, knit to end of rnd).
Rnd 26 (in CC): Purl.
Rnds 27–51: Rep rnds 2–26 (1 time).
Rnd 52 (in CC): Knit.
Rnd 53 (in CC): Purl.

Rnd 54 (in MC): Knit.
Rnd 55 (in MC): Purl.
Rnd 56 (in MC): Knit.
Rnds 57–58 (in MC): Rep rnds 55–56 (1 time).
Chain one bind-off all sts.

Finishing

Weave in all ends. Block cowl by gently stretching it height-wise until knitting lies flat; do not stretch cowl horizontally unless you would like your cowl to sit loosely around your neck. Blocking is necessary to remove puckering caused by the short rows.

Flourish Tote Bag

Carry all that you need in this elegant, medium-size tote. It's worked as one piece with two side seams, using 100 percent wool. Wooden handles, tassels, and a linen liner add the final touches to this useful and pretty bag.

Level

Confident Beginner

Finished Measurements

13 in/33 cm wide x 14 in/35.6 cm long

Gauge

18 sts and 32 rows = 4 in/10.2 cm square in stockinette stitch

Yarn

Patons Classic Wool Worsted, worsted weight #4 (100% wool; 210 yd/192 m, 3.5 oz/100 g per skein)
1 skein #00201 Winter White (A)
2 skeins #00230 Bright Red (B)

Supplies

- 3/8 in/1 cm peg spacing loom with at least 60 pegs
- Knitting tool
- Crochet hook
- Yarn/tapestry needle
- 2 wood handles (those shown by Everything Mary)
- ***Optional:*** 1/2 yd/.45 m fabric for lining tote (100% linen used in sample)

Pattern Notes

- In a hurry? Omit the Fair Isle pattern and knit those rows in a coordinating solid color for an easy and fast tote project. The large stripe will add interest!
- Tote is worked as one piece and then folded in half and seamed up the sides.
- When doing the Fair Isle portion, carry the nonworking yarn, catching it every 2 stitches by laying it on top of the working yarn. This will keep the front of your stitches tidy. For photo-illustrated instructions on how to carry yarn when working Fair Isle, see page 126.

Pattern

TOP OF TOTE (FIRST HALF)

Foundation row: Chain CO 60 pegs with 1 strand Color B; work as flat panel.

Row 1: *K2, p1, rep from * to end.

Row 2: *P1, k2, rep from * to end.

Rows 3–12: Rep rows 1 and 2 (5 times).

Rows 13–76: Knit.

FAIR ISLE SECTION (CHART WORKS FROM BOTTOM, RIGHT CORNER)

Row 1: K60 in B. (60 sts)

Row 2: [K1 in B, k2 in A, k5 in B, k2 in A, k2 in B] 5 times. (60 sts)

Row 3: [K1 in B, k1 in A, (k2 in B, k1 in A, k1 in B) twice, k1 in B, k1 in A] 5 times. (60 sts)

Row 4: [K1 in A, k3 in B, k1 in A, k1 in B] 10 times. (60 sts)

Row 5: [K2 in B, (k2 in A, k1 in B, k1 in A) twice, k1 in A, k1 in B] 5 times. (60 sts)

Row 6: [K5 in B, k1 in A, k6 in B] 5 times. (60 sts)

Row 7: [K1 in B, k1 in A, k3 in B, k1 in A] 10 times. (60 sts)

Row 8: [K1 in B, k3 in A, k3 in B, k3 in A, k1 in B, k1 in A] 5 times. (60 sts)

Row 9: [K1 in B, k1 in A, k3 in B, k1 in A] 10 times. (60 sts)

Row 10: [K5 in B, k1 in A, k6 in B] 5 times. (60 sts)

Row 11: [K2 in B, k2 in A, (k2 in B, k1 in A) twice, k1 in A, k1 in B] 5 times. (60 sts)

Row 12: [K1 in A, k3 in B, k1 in A, k1 in B] 10 times. (60 sts)

Row 13: [K1 in B, k1 in A, (k2 in B, k1 in A, k1 in B) twice, k1 in B, k1 in A] 5 times. (60 sts)

Row 14: [K1 in B, k2 in A, k5 in B, k2 in A, k2 in B] 5 times. (60 sts)

Rows 15–28: Rep rows 1–14 (1 time).

Rows 29–44: Knit in B.

Rows 45–72: Rep rows 1–14 of Fair Isle pattern (2 times).

TOP OF TOTE (SECOND HALF)

Rows 1–64: Knit in B.

Rows 65–76: Rep ribbing rows 1 and 2 from first half Top of Tote 6 times in Color B.

Chain one bind-off, leaving a long tail for seaming side of bag.

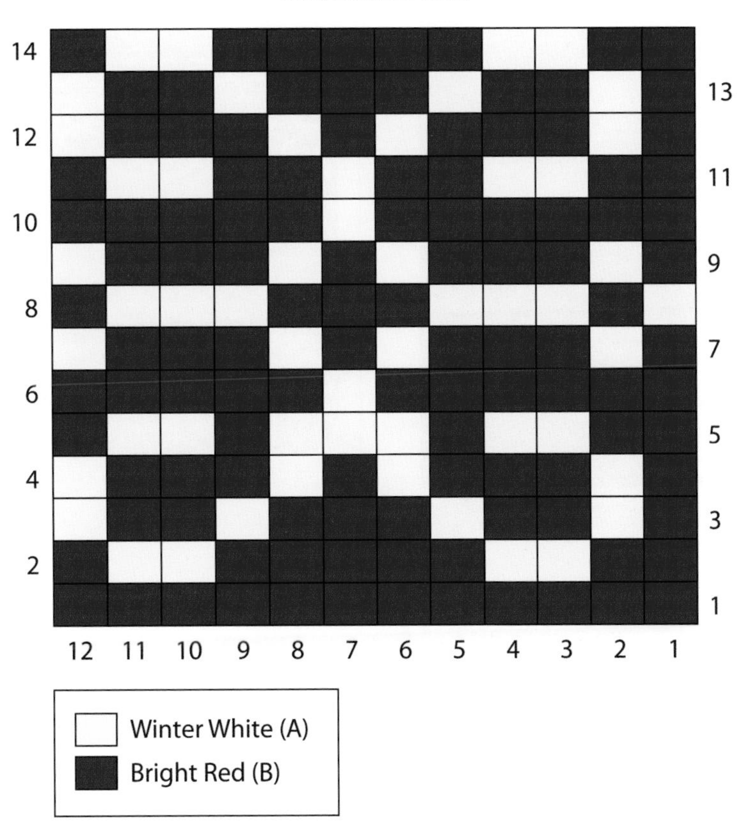

Finishing

Fold the bag in half and mattress stitch sides of bag. Weave in ends. Center the handle on front of bag and secure. Rep for back of the bag. Line the bag with fabric (optional). Braid 3 strands of Color A (5 in/12.7 cm long) and knot the ends to secure. Make and attach a 5 in/12.7 cm tassel to each end of braid.

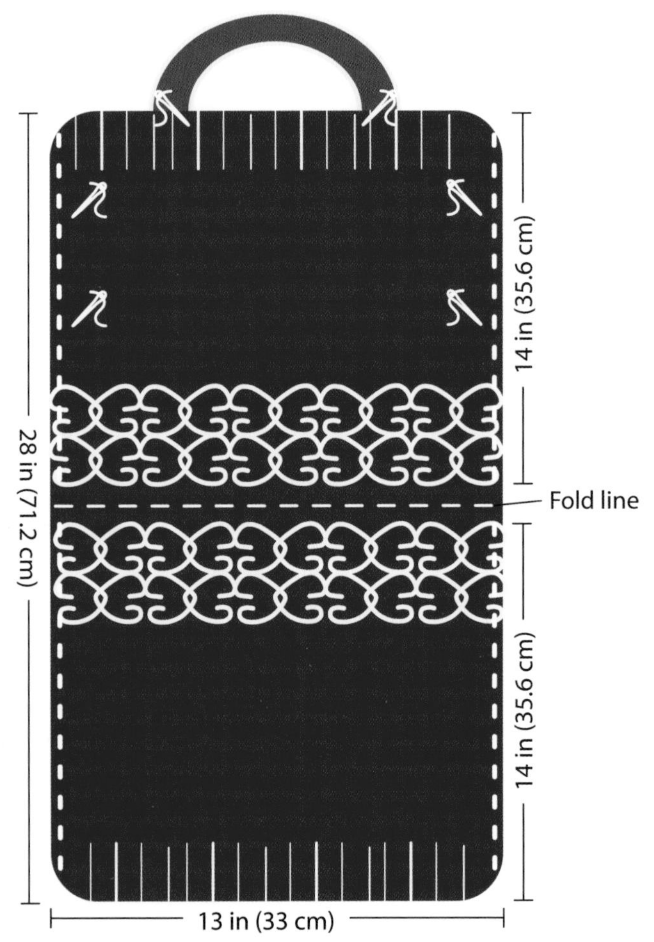

Cocoon Cowl

A hybrid of a cowl and vest, this accessory can be dressed up or down. It has unusual construction, made up of three triangles, and a cable accent recessed in purl stitches. Two final straps are added to the back portion, pulling it all together.

Level

Intermediate

Finished Measurements

Approximately 46 in/116.8 cm around chest and 19 in/48.3 cm high

One size fits most.

Gauge

17 sts and 28 rows = 4 in/10.2 cm square in stockinette stitch. Take time to check gauge.

Yarn

Lion Brand Heartland Yarn, worsted weight #4 (100% acrylic; 251 yd/230 m, 5 oz/142 g per skein)
5 skeins #136-149 Great Smoky Mountains

Supplies

- 3/8 in/1 cm peg spacing loom with 90 pegs
- Knitting tool
- Crochet hook
- 2 stitch markers
- Measuring tape
- Yarn/tapestry needle

Special Stitches

4-st RC (4-stitch right cross): Place the stitches from pegs 1 and 2 onto cable needles and position them to the inside of the loom, behind the pegs. Knit peg 3, and then move the stitch to peg 1. Knit peg 4, and then move it to peg 2. Transfer the stitch from peg 1 being held on a cable needle to peg 3, and transfer the stitch from peg 2 being held on a cable needle to peg 4. Knit pegs 3 and 4.

Pattern Notes

- 3 triangles and 2 straps are worked and then seamed together to form cowl.
- Use the regular knit stitch to achieve gauge; the u-knit will create a smaller garment.
- Knitting is designed to roll at the edges, giving it a unique drape and allowing the garment to hug the body.
- For photo-illustrated instructions on how to work the 4-st RC, see page 117.

Pattern

TRIANGLE A

Place stitch markers on pegs 38 and 51. You will work the cable detail between these markers. Do not skip this step.

HEM

Foundation row: Chain CO 90 pegs; work as flat panel.
Row 1: Knit
Rep row 1 until knitting measures 2½ in/6.4 cm.
Turn up hem by lifting the first row of sts up onto the loom, being careful to keep stitch rows straight.

CABLE PATTERN

Rows 1–4: Knit to 1st marker, [p2, k4] twice, p2, knit to end of row.
Row 5: Knit to 1st marker, [p2, 4-st RC] twice, p2, knit to end of row.
Rows 6–30: Rep rows 1–5 (5 times).
Row 31: K2tog, knit to 1st marker, [p2, k4] twice, p2, knit to last 2 sts, ssk. (88 sts)
Rows 32–34: Knit to 1st marker, [p2, k4] twice, p2, knit to end of row.
Row 35: Knit to 1st marker, [p2, 4-st RC] twice, p2, knit to end of row.
Rows 36–75: Rep rows 31–35 (8 times). (72 sts)
Row 76: K2tog, knit to 1st marker, [p2, k4] twice, p2, knit to last 2 sts, ssk. (70 sts)
Rows 77–79: Knit to 1st marker, [p2, k4] twice, p2, knit to end of row.
Row 80: Knit to 1st marker, [p2, 4-st RC] twice, p2, knit to end of row.
Rows 81–84: Knit to 1st marker, [p2, k4] twice, p2, knit to end of row.
Row 85: Knit to 1st marker, [p2, 4-st RC] twice, p2, knit to end of row.
Rows 86–145: Rep rows 76–85 (6 times). (58 sts)
Row 146: K2tog, knit to 1st marker, [p2, k4] twice, p2, knit to last 2 sts, ssk. (56 sts)
Row 147: Knit to 1st marker, [p2, k4] twice, p2, knit to end of row.
Row 148: As row 148. (54 sts)
Row 149: As row 149.
Row 150: K2tog, knit to 1st marker, [p2, 4-st RC] twice, p2, knit to last 2 sts, ssk. (52 sts)
Row 151: Knit to 1st marker, [p2, k4] twice, p2, knit to end of row.
Row 152: K2tog, knit to 1st marker, [p2, k4] twice, p2, knit to last 2 sts, ssk. (50 sts)
Row 153: Knit to 1st marker, [p2, k4] twice, p2, knit to end of row.
Row 154: As row 154. (48 sts)
Row 155: Knit to 1st marker, [p2, 4-st RC] twice, p2, knit to end of row.
Rows 156–175: Rep rows 146–155 (2 times). (28 sts)
Rows 176–182: Rep rows 146–152 (1 time). (20 sts)
Chain one bind-off 20 sts.

TRIANGLE B

Foundation row: Chain CO 90 sts; work as flat panel.
Row 1: Knit.
Rep row 1 until knitting measures 2½ in/6.4 cm.
Turn up hem by lifting the first row of sts up onto the loom, being careful to keep stitch rows straight.
Rows 1–116: Knit.
Row 117: K2tog, knit to last 2 sts, ssk. (88 sts)
Row 118: Knit.
Rep rows 117 and 118 until there are 20 sts left on the loom.
Chain one bind-off all sts.

TRIANGLE C

Foundation row: Chain CO 45 pegs; work as flat panel.
Rows 1–157: Knit.
Row 158: K2tog, knit to last 2 sts, ssk. (43 sts)
Row 159: Knit.
Rep rows 158 and 159 until there are 19 sts left on the loom.

BACK STRAPS (MAKE 2)

Foundation row: Chain CO 10 sts; work as flat panel.
Row 1: Knit.
Rep row 1 until strap measures 8½ in/21.6 cm.
Chain one bind-off.

Finishing

Weave in ends. With right sides facing up, place the hem of Triangle A on top of the hem of Triangle B, and seam together. Seam Triangle C to Triangle A 12 in/30.5 cm from where hem ends. Seam the narrow end of Triangle B to the side of Triangle A 4½ in/11.4 cm from top edge (yellow dots on schematic). Seam the two straps 1 in/2.5 cm apart onto the side of Triangle C, 5 in/12.7 cm from where Triangles A and C meet (green dots). Seam the narrow end of Triangle C to the side of Triangle B beginning just below the hem (blue dots on schematic). Seam the other side of straps to Triangle B, starting 5 in/12.7 cm from seam at narrow end (green dots).

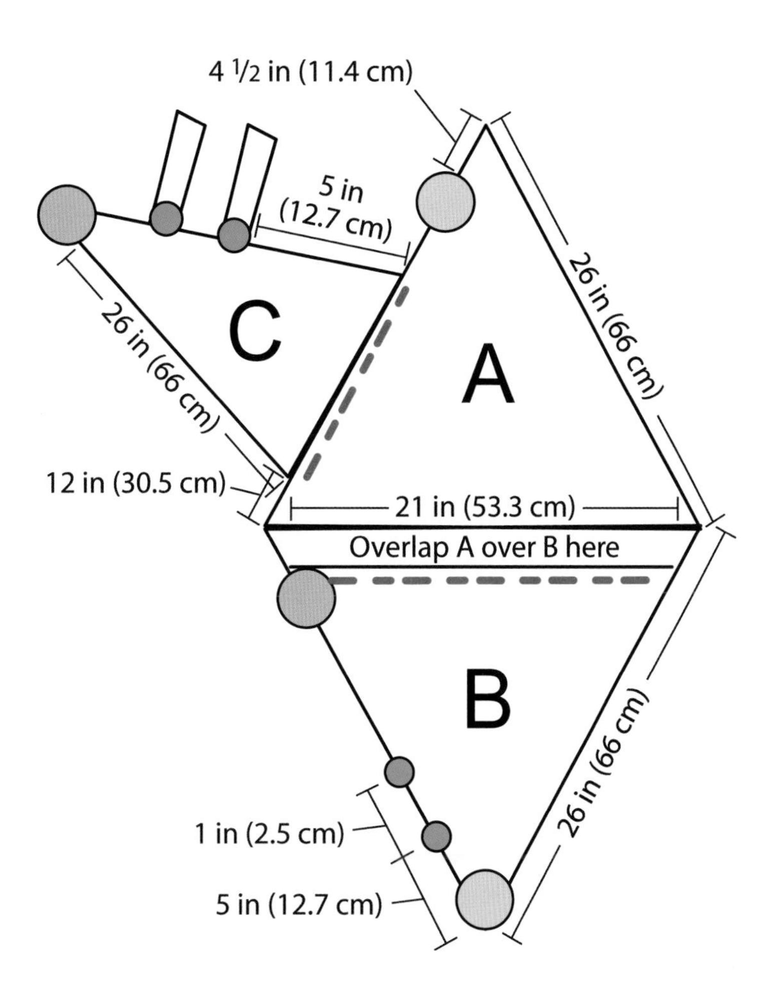

Convertible Mitts

Rugged with a touch of alpaca softness, these mitts will keep you warm on the coldest of days. They provide the warmth of a mitten with the practicality of a fingerless mitt. A button keeps the hood in place when not in use. These are a quick loom knit and would make a great last-minute gift idea!

Level

Beginner

Finished Measurements

Approximately 10½ in/26.7 cm long x 8 in/20.3 cm circumference. Total length includes hood and is measured after assembly.

Gauge

12 sts and 22 rows = 4 in/10.2 cm in stockinette stitch

Yarn

Yarn Bee Brushworks, light worsted #3 (80% acrylic, 20% alpaca; 254 yd/233 m, 3.5 oz/100 g per skein)
1 skein #09 Mocha (MC)
1 skein #03 Red (CC)

Supplies

- ⅝ in/1.6 cm peg spacing round loom with 24 pegs
- Knitting tool
- Crochet hook
- Measuring tape
- Yarn/tapestry needle
- 2 wood buttons

Pattern Notes

- Main mitt is worked in one piece in the round. The hood for the mitt is worked as a separate piece and seamed to the back of the main mitt.
- Mitt is knit in one size with slight decreasing at the top of mitt for a snug fit. You may leave out the decreases if you have large hands.
- The thumb is worked as two separate pieces attached at the bottom of the thumb to the main glove. Later you will seam both sides of the thumb closed, leaving the tip and bottom open for the thumb to be inserted.

Main Mitt (make 2)

Foundation round: Chain CO all 24 pegs with 1 strand MC; join to work in the round.
Rnds 1–3: *K1, p1, rep from * to end of round.
Rnd 4 (in CC): Knit.
Rnds 5–6 (in CC): *K1, p1, rep from * to end of round.
Rnd 7 (in MC): Knit.
Rnds 8–9 (in MC): *K1, p1, rep from * to end of round.
Rnds 10–12 (in CC): Rep rnds 4 through 6 (1 time). (24 sts)
Cut CC (leave a tail for weaving) and work in MC only.
Rnd 13: Knit.
Rnds 14–22: *K1, p1, rep from * to end of round.
Rnds 23–35: Knit.

THUMB

Stop knitting in the round and knit over 6 pegs only.

First Side of Thumb

Rows 1–10: Knit.
Row 11: (K1, p1) 3 times.
Row 12: (P1, k1) 3 times.
Row 13: As row 11.
Chain one bind-off 6 pegs.

Second Side of Thumb

Chain CO 6 pegs. These pegs will now be empty after working the first side of the thumb.
Row 1: (K1, p1) 3 times.
Row 2: (P1, k1) 3 times.
Row 3: As row 11.
Rows 4–13: Knit.
Do not bind off; begin knitting in the round.

TOP OF MITT

Rnds 1–5: Knit in MC. (24 sts)
Rnds 6–8: Knit in CC.
Rnds 9–11: Knit in MC.
Rnds 12–14: Knit in CC.
Cut CC; work in MC only. If leaving out decreases, work 1x1 rib for rows 15–18 instead of decreases as follows.
Rnd 15: Knit. (24 sts)
Stop knitting in the round. Knit as flat panel and change directions at the end of each row.
Row 16: K2tog, *k1, p1, rep from * to last 2 sts, ssk. (22 sts)
Row 17: *K1, p1, rep from * to end of row.
Row 18: K2tog, *p1, k1, rep from * to last 2 sts, ssk. (20 sts)
Row 19: K2, *p1, k1, rep from * to end.
Chain one bind-off all pegs and leave a long tail for seaming the top of your mitt closed.

Mitt Hood (make 2)

Foundation round: Chain CO all 24 pegs with 2 strands CC; join to work in the round.
Rnds 1–3: *K1, p1, rep from * to end of round.
Cut CC and work in MC only.
Rnds 4–23: Knit in MC.
Bind off using gather method (see page 112).
Weave in ends.

Finishing

Seam the top, side of your mitt closed. Weave in all ends and seam the sides of your thumb closed using mattress stitch.

Place mitt on hand, place hood over fingers and line up the top stripe of mitt with the stripe on hood (see illustration). Pin in place and sew along bottom of stripe. Begin seaming along one side of hand, across the back of hand, and finish on the opposite side. Wrapping your seam around the sides of your hand will ensure a snug fit. Do not seam palm side of hood to mitt. Fold the hood back, and make a loop large enough to go over your button. You may use a single strand of yarn (as shown in the sample), an I-cord, or braid to make loop. Secure the loop. Line up the button and the loop and sew on your button.

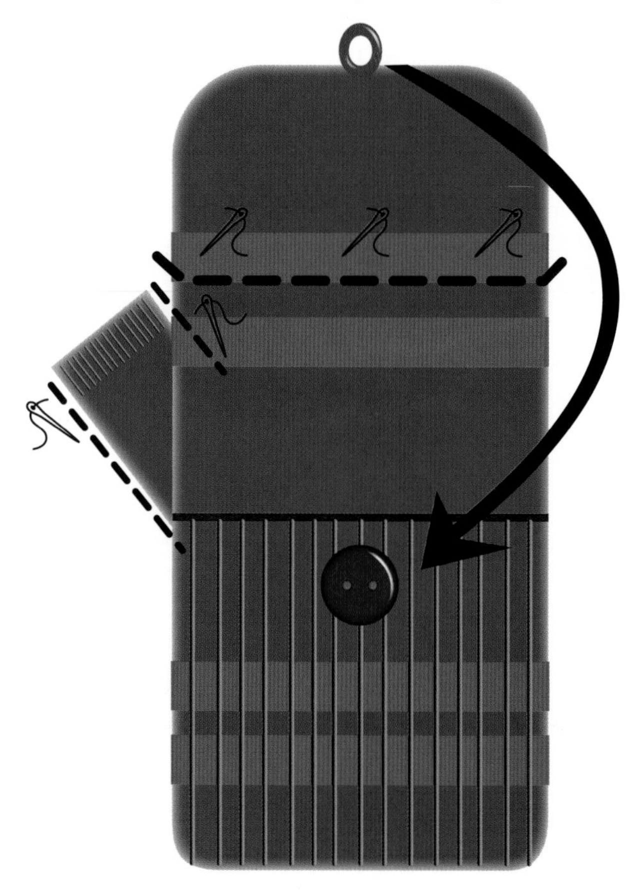

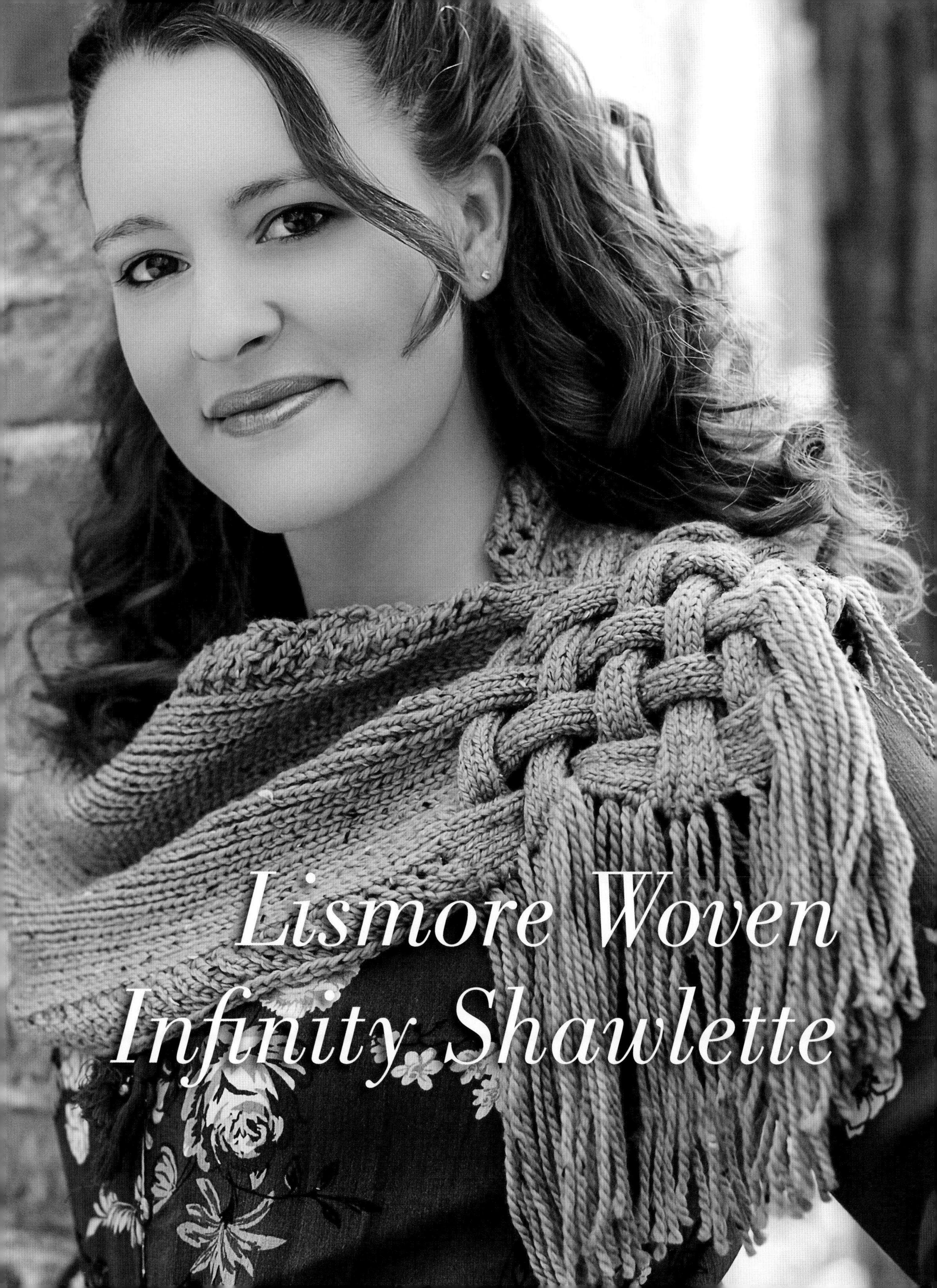

Lismore Woven Infinity Shawlette

This shawlette is a real head-turner, featuring a woven knot, a fisherman's rib, and a diagonal eyelet border. Wear it over an outfit or heavy winter coat.

Level

Confident Beginner

Finished Measurements

40 in/101.6 cm circumference (adjustable to suit) x 11 in/27.9 cm, after blocking

Gauge

20 sts and 28 rows = 4 in/10.2 cm square in fisherman's rib stitch

Yarn

Plymouth Yarn Homestead Tweed, Aran weight #4 (90% wool, 10% Donegal; 191 yd/175 m, 3.5 oz/100 g per skein)

2 skeins #525 Pale Moss Tweed

Supplies

- ⅜ in/1 cm peg spacing loom with 35 pegs
- Knitting tool
- Crochet hook
- Yarn/tapestry needle
- Measuring tape

Special Stitches

sh3-yo (shift 3, yarn over): Takes place over the first 4 stitches at the beginning of a row, shifting 3 stitches toward the outside edge. Move the stitch from peg 2 to peg 1. Move the stitch from peg 3 to peg 2. Move the stitch from peg 4 to peg 3. Knit 2 together on peg 1, knit pegs 2 and 3, e-wrap peg 4 (yarn over) but do not knit.

Skip1 wyif: Skip one peg by placing the working yarn in front of the peg. Do not work this peg.

TK: Tuck knit. Use the regular knit stitch to knit all sts together on this peg. This will include the yarn over made by the skip1 wyif on the previous row.

yo-sh3 (yarn over, shift 3): Takes place over the last 4 stitches of a row, shifting toward the outside edge. Move the stitch from peg 3 to peg 4, the outside peg. Move the stitch from peg 2 to peg 3. Move the stitch from peg 1 to peg 2. E-wrap peg 1 (yarn over) but do not knit, knit pegs 2 and 3, knit 2 together on peg 4.

Pattern Notes

- Fisherman's rib is worked similarly to brioche stitch on the loom, but all pegs are knit, no purls.
- Scarf is worked in 5 separate sections at the beginning and end and then woven together, forming one piece.
- For photo-illustrated instructions on how to work the sh3-yo and yo-sh3, see pages 118–19.

ROI
JOIE.

Pattern

FIRST FIVE SECTIONS

Foundation row: Chain CO 7 pegs.

Row 1: Knit.

Rep row 1 until work measures 6 in/15.25 cm, keeping track of rows to ensure all sections are equal for all sections.

Cut yarn but do not bind off.

Rep above 4 more times, completing a total of 5 adjacent sections. On the fifth section do not cut yarn.

MAIN SCARF

Row 1: Knit. (35 sts)

Row 2: Sh3-yo, k1, [skip1 wyif, k1] 13 times, yo-sh3.

Row 3: K4, skip1 wyif, [TK, skip1 wyif] 13 times, k4.

Row 4: K4, TK, [skip1 wyif, TK] 13 times, k4.

Row 5: Sh3-yo, skip1 wyif, [TK, skip1 wyif] 13 times, yo-sh3.

Rep rows 3–5 until total work (including straps for knot) measures 40 in/101.6 cm. This measurement can be lengthened or shortened for perfect fit. Measure around chest and shoulders; then subtract 6 in/15.25 cm for knot. *Tip:* If you wish to wear it over a heavy coat, measure with the coat on.

Next row: Knit. (35 sts)

FIVE SECTIONS AT OTHER END

Begin working in sections over 7 pegs/sts each.

Row 1: K7.

Rep row 1 until work measures 6 in/15.25 cm, keeping track of rows to ensure all sections are equal. Rows should also equal first 5 sections.

Bind off, leaving a long tail for seaming later.

Rep above 4 more times, completing a total of 5 adjacent sections.

Finishing

Weave end sections in and out—see illustration for placement—seaming just the ends together to secure. Weave in all ends. Attach 7.5 in/19 cm fringe to the bottom edges of the woven area.

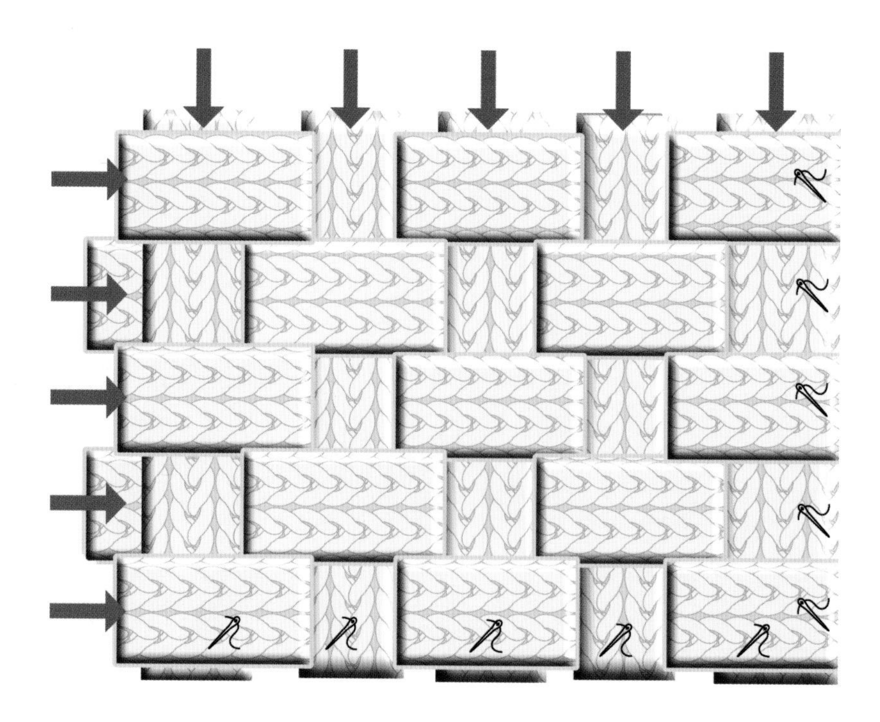

Shetland Leg Warmers

Although these leg warmers require a time investment, the resulting beauty will be well worth the effort. With proper care, you will be able to hand them down from generation to generation.

Level

Confident Beginner

Sizes/Finished Measurements

Sizes: Large adult ladies (medium/small adult ladies, child). Instructions are written for size large adult ladies, with other sizes in parentheses. When only one instruction is given, it applies to all sizes.

Length: 18¼ (18¼, 16¼) in/46.4 (46.4, 41.3) cm (length may be adjusted as desired)

Circumference: 15 (13, 11) in/38.1 (33, 27.9) cm

Gauge

20 sts and 28 rows = 4 in/10.2 cm in 1x1 rib stitch

20 sts and 26 rows = 4 in/10.2 cm in stockinette stitch

Yarn

Knit Picks Wool of The Andes, worsted weight #4 (100% Peruvian Highland Wool; 110 yd/100.6 m, 1.76 oz/50 g per skein)

2 skeins #25639 Bouquet Heather (MC)
1 skein #25651 Turmeric (A)
1 skein #24279 Mink Heather (B)
1 skein #24074 Pampas Heather (C)
1 skein #25642 Rooibos Heather (D)
1 skein #25635 Cilantro Heather (E)
1 skein #24280 Persimmon Heather (F)
1 skein #24071 Claret Heather (G)

Supplies

- ⅜ in/1 cm peg spacing round loom with 72 (large adult), 60 (medium/small adult), or 48 (child) pegs
- Knitting tool
- Crochet hook
- Measuring tape

Pattern Notes

- Leg warmers are knit in the round from the top down.
- Fair Isle chart works in multiples of 12 sts.
- If knitting child's size, you will need to measure the child's leg (knee to ankle) and adjust row count for the Fair Isle portion of the warmer as needed.
- For photo-illustrated instructions on working Fair Isle colorwork, see page 126.

Pattern

Foundation round: Chain CO 72 (60, 48) pegs with 1 strand MC; join to work in the rnd.

TOP RIBBING

Rnd 1: *K1, p1, rep from * to end of round.

Rep rnd 1 until total work measures 4 (4, 3¼) in/10.2 (10.2, 8.3) cm.

FAIR ISLE CHART

The rounds below represent the 12 sts of the Fair Isle chart. You will work these 12 sts 6 (5, 4) times each round.

Rnd 1: [K1 in G, k5 in B] twice.
Rnd 2: [K1 in B, k1 in G, k3 in B, k1 in G] twice.
Rnd 3: [K1 in G, k2 in B] 4 times.
Rnd 4: [K2 in B, k3 in G, k1 in B] twice.
Rnd 5: [K1 in B, k2 in G] 4 times.
Rnd 6: [K2 in G, k3 in B, k1 in G] twice.
Rnds 7–10: Rep rnds 3–6.
Rnd 11: [K1 in G, k2 in B] 4 times.
Rnd 12: [K2 in B, (k1 in G, k1 in B) twice] twice.
Rnd 13: [K3 in B, k1 in G, k2 in B] twice.
Rnd 14: K12 in A.
Rnd 15: K2 in E, k7 in A, k2 in E, k1 in A.
Rnd 16: [K2 in A, k1 in E] 4 times.
Rnd 17: K2 in A, [k1 in E, k1 in A] 4 times, k2 in A.
Rnd 18: [(K1 in A, k1 in E) twice, k2 in A] twice.
Rnd 19: [K1 in E, k1 in A] twice, k4 in A, [k1 in E, k1 in A] twice.
Rnd 20: [K2 in A, k1 in E] 4 times.
Rnd 21: K3 in A, [k2 in E, k1 in A] twice, k3 in A.
Rnd 22: K12 in A.
Rnd 23: [K1 in C, k1 in D, k2 in C] 3 times.
Rnd 24: [K3 in D, k1 in C] 3 times.
Rnd 25: K1 in C, [k1 in D, k1 in C, k1 in D] 3 times, k1 in C, k1 in D.
Rnd 26: K1 in D, k1 in C, k2 in D, k2 in C, [k1 in C, k2 in D] twice.
Rnd 27: K1 in C, k2 in D, [k2 in C, k1 in D] twice, k1 in D, k1 in C, k1 in D.
Rnd 28: [K2 in D, k2 in C, k1 in D] twice, k1 in D, k1 in C.
Rnd 29: K1 in C, k2 in D, [k2 in C, k1 in D] twice, k1 in D, k1 in C, k1 in D.
Rnd 30: K1 in D, k1 in C, k2 in D, k2 in C, [k1 in C, k2 in D] twice.
Rnd 31: K1 in C, [k1 in D, k1 in C, k1 in D] 3 times, k1 in C, k1 in D.
Rnd 32: [K3 in D, k1 in C] 3 times.
Rnd 33: [K1 in C, k1 in D, k2 in C] 3 times.
Rnd 34: K12 in F.
Rnd 35: [K2 in F, k1 in B] 4 times.
Rnd 36: [K1 in F, k3 in B, k2 in F] twice.
Rnd 37: [K2 in B, k1 in F] 4 times.
Rnd 38: [K1 in B, k3 in F, k2 in B] twice.
Rnd 39: [K2 in F, k1 in B] 4 times.

Rnd 40: K12 in F.
Rnd 41: [K2 in G, k3 in B, k1 in G] twice.
Rnd 42: [K1 in G, k1 in B, k3 in G, k1 in B] twice.
Rnd 43: [K1 in B, k2 in G] 4 times.
Rnd 44: [K2 in G, k3 in B, k1 in G] twice.
Rnd 45: [K1 in B, k2 in G] 4 times.
Rnd 46: [K1 in G, k1 in B, k3 in G, k1 in B] twice.
Rnd 47: [K2 in G, k3 in B, k1 in G] twice.
Rnd 48: K12 in G.
Rnd 49: [K2 in E, k1 in A, k3 in E] twice.
Rnd 50: K1 in E, k3 in A, k3 in E, [k1 in A, k1 in E] twice, k1 in E.
Rnd 51: [K2 in E, k1 in A, k1 in E] twice, [k1 in A, k1 in E] twice.
Rnd 52: K4 in E, [k1 in E, k1 in A] 4 times.
Rnd 53: [K1 in A, k3 in E, k1 in A, k1 in E] twice.
Rnd 54: [K1 in E, k1 in A] 3 times, k5 in E, k1 in A.
Rnd 55: [K1 in A, k1 in E] twice, [k1 in A, k3 in E] twice.
Rnd 56: [K1 in E, k1 in A] twice, k3 in E, k3 in A, k2 in E.
Rnd 57: [K2 in E, k1 in A, k3 in E] twice.
Rnd 58: K12 in D.
Rnd 59: [K1 in D, k1 in C] 6 times.
Rnd 60: K12 in D.
Rep chart until total work measures 16½ (16½, 15) in/42 (42, 38.1) cm (or desired length less ribbing).

BOTTOM RIBBING

Rnd 1: With MC, knit.
Rnd 2: *K1, p1, rep from * to end of round.
Rep rnd 2 until bottom ribbing measures 1¾ (1¾, 1¼) in/4.4 (4.4, 3.2) cm.
Chain one bind-off all sts.

Finishing

Weave in ends and block lightly. Do not stretch ribbing during blocking.

FAIR ISLE CHART

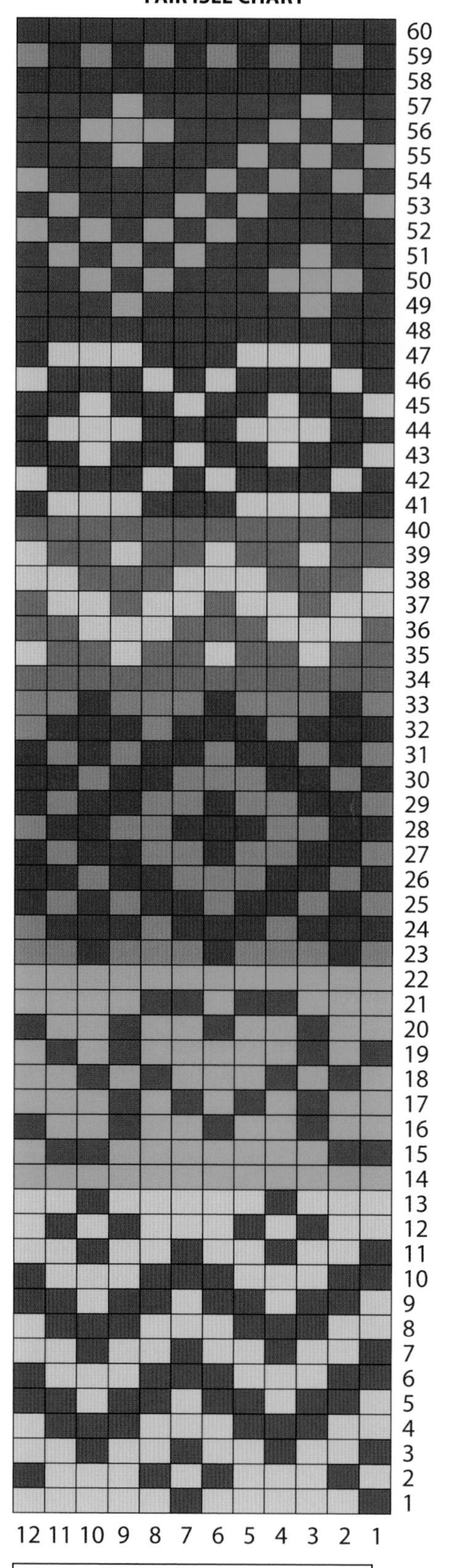

Gansey Beanie

Gansey stitch patterns are a combination of knits and purls that create lovely, lofty texture in the knitted fabric. Although traditionally used for fisherman-type sweaters, gansey stitch patterns look good on hats and scarves too. This hat will introduce you to a sampling of gansey stitches.

Level

Beginner

Finished Measurements

9 in/22.9 cm tall x 20 in/50.8 cm circumference (when stretched)

To fit adult/teen.

Gauge

17 sts and 49 rows = 4 in/10.2 cm in gansey stitch pattern

Yarn

Lion Brand Scarfie, bulky weight #5 (78% acrylic, 22% wool; 312 yd/285 m, 5.3 oz/150 g per skein)
1 skein #206 Cream/Taupe

Supplies

- 3/8 in/1 cm peg spacing round loom with 80 pegs
- Knitting tool
- Crochet hook

Pattern Notes

- You may do any combination of the gansey pattern stitches until your hat measures desired length. It is recommended to end the top of the hat in 1x1 rib to help "pull in" the top of the hat, as gansey stitches can be bulky.
- Each gansey stitch pattern is separated with 2 purl rows to create a ridge in the fabric.
- You may use the regular knit or u-knit to complete this hat. Leave 1½ in/3.8 cm at the top of hat for ribbing. Sample hat was completed using the u-knit and all the pattern sts in the order listed.
- Cast-on edge of brim is designed to roll slightly.
- For photo-illustrated instructions on how to work the u-knit stitch and how to bind off with the gather method, see pages 114 and 112.

Pattern

Foundation round: Chain CO 80 pegs; join to work in the round.
Rnds 1–5: Knit.

FIRST GANSEY STITCH (1X1 RIBBING, MULTIPLES OF 2)

Rnds 1–8: *K1, p1, rep from * to end of round.
Rnds 9–10: Purl.

SECOND PATTERN STITCH (DIAGONAL STITCH, MULTIPLES OF 8)

Rnds 1–8: *K2, p1, rep from * to end of round. Continue this pattern without interruption from round to round. This will push your purl stitch forward by 1 stitch on each round. Stay in sequence until the last stitch on rnd 8.
Rnds 9–10: Purl.

THIRD PATTERN STITCH (STAMEN PATTERN, MULTIPLES OF 2)

Rnd 1: Knit.
Rnd 2: *P1, skip1 wyif, rep from * to end of round.
Rnd 3: Knit.
Rnd 4: *Skip1 wyif, p1, rep from * to end of round.
Rnds 5–8: Rep rnds 1–4.
Rnd 9: Knit.
Rnds 10–11: Purl.

FOURTH PATTERN STITCH (MOCK WEAVE, MULTIPLES OF 4)

Rnd 1: Knit.
Rnd 2: *K2, p2, rep from * to end of round.
Rnds 3–8: Rep rnds 1 and 2 (3 times).
Rnd 9: Knit.
Rnds 10 and 11: Purl.

FIFTH PATTERN STITCH (MULTIPLES OF 4)

Rnds 1–2: *K2, p2, rep from * to end of round.
Rnds 3–4: *P2, k2, rep from * to end of round.
Rnds 5–6: As rnds 1 and 2.
Rnds 7–8: As rnds 3 and 4.
Rnds 9–10: Purl.

SIXTH PATTERN STITCH (SEED STITCH, MULTIPLES OF 2)

Rnd 1: *K1, p1, rep from * to end of round.
Rnd 2: *P1, k1, rep from * to end of round.
Rnds 3–8: Rep rnds 1 and 2 (3 times).
Rnds 9–10: Purl.

SEVENTH PATTERN STITCH (STAGGERED ARROWS, MULTIPLES OF 8)

Rnd 1: *K1, p1, k5, p1, rep from * to end of round.
Rnd 2: *[K2, p1, k1] twice, rep from * to end of round.
Rnd 3: *K3 [p1, k1] twice, k1, rep from * to end of round.
Rnd 4: *K4, p1, k3, rep from * to end of round.
Rnds 5–8: Rep rnds 1–4.
Rnds 9–10: Purl.

EIGHTH PATTERN STITCH (MISTAKE RIB, MULTIPLES OF 4)

Rnd 1: *K1, p1, rep from * to end of round.
Rnd 2: Knit.
Rnds 3–8: Rep rnds 1 and 2 (3 times).
Rnds 9–10: Purl.

NINTH PATTERN STITCH (CORNER STITCH, MULTIPLES OF 8 STS)

Rnd 1: Knit.
Rnd 2: *[K1, p3] twice, rep from * to end of round.
Rnds 3–4: *[K1, p1, k2] twice, rep from * to end of round.
Rnd 5: Knit.
Rnd 6: *[K1, p3] twice, rep from * to end of round.
Rnds 7–8: *[K1, p1, k2] twice, rep from * to end of round.
Rnd 9: Knit.
Rnds 10–11: Purl.

TOP OF HAT

Rnds 1–8: *K1, p1, rep from * to end of round.
Bind off using the gather method.

Finishing

Weave in ends. Blocking is not necessary.

Argyle Mittens

The slim fit and Argyle design give these mittens a vintage feel. The Fair Isle pattern is beautiful and creates a double thickness to the knit fabric, making these mittens extra warm.

Level

Intermediate

Finished Measurements

Fits up to 8½ in/21.6 cm circumference, ladies/teen size. Mitten is 10½ in/26.7 cm long.

Gauge

20 sts and 28 rows = 4 in/10.2 cm in stockinette stitch

Yarn

Knit Picks Swish Worsted, worsted weight #4 (100% fine superwash merino wool; 110 yd/100.5 m, 1.75 oz/50 g per skein)

1 skein #25153 Marble Heather (A)
1 skein #25143 Cornmeal (B)

Supplies

- ⅜ in/1 cm peg spacing round loom with 36 pegs
- Knitting tool
- Yarn/tapestry needle
- Crochet hook
- Measuring tape

Stitch Pattern

Argyle Pattern (12-stitch repeat over 36 sts)

Rnd 1: [K3 in A, k1 in B, k2 in A] 6 times.

Rnd 2: [K2 in A, k3 in B, k3 in A, (k1 in B, k1 in A) twice] 3 times.

Rnd 3: [K1 in A, k4 in B, (k1 in B, k1 in A) twice, k2 in A, k1 in B] 3 times.

Rnd 4: [K1 in B, k1 in A, k2 in B, (k1 in B, k1 in A) twice, k4 in A] 3 times.

Rnd 5: [K2 in B, (k1 in A, k1 in B) twice, k2 in B, k3 in A, k1 in B] 3 times.

Rnd 6: [K3 in B, k1 in A, k2 in B] 6 times.

Rnd 7: [K2 in B, (k1 in A, k1 in B) twice, k2 in B, k3 in A, k1 in B] 3 times.

Rnd 8: [K1 in B, k1 in A, k2 in B, (k1 in B, k1 in A) twice, k4 in A] 3 times.

Rnd 9: [K1 in A, k4 in B, (k1 in B, k1 in A) twice, k2 in A, k1 in B] 3 times.

Rnd 10: [K2 in A, k3 in B, k3 in A, (k1 in B, k1 in A) twice] 3 times.

Pattern Notes

- Mittens are knit in the round from the bottom up.
- Thumb is worked flat by knitting one long piece of knitting that will naturally fold over at the tip of the thumb. You will then resume knitting in the round.
- Thumb is seamed on the sides, to close, after mitten is complete.
- Carry your yarn to avoid long floats inside the mittens, twisting the colors together as necessary (see page 126 on how to work Fair Isle colorwork, Method 2). Mittens can also be lined with fleece after finishing, if desired.

Pattern

Foundation round: Chain CO 36 sts with 1 strand A; join to work in the round.

Rnd 1: *K2, p2, rep from * to end of round.

Rep rnd 1 until work measures 4 in/10.2 cm.

BODY OF MITTEN

Rnd 1: Knit all sts in A, continuing to knit in the round.

Rnds 2–5: Work rnds 1–4 of Argyle pattern in Colors A and B.

Begin Thumb

Stop knitting in the round. Work thumb in A, in short rows over 7 pegs (add a peg if you have a wider thumb).

Row 1: Knit in A.

Rep row 1 until thumb measures 5 in/12.7 cm. Adjust thumb length to suit by measuring your thumb length (hand to tip of thumb) and then double that number.

Begin knitting in the round again.

Resume Body Knitting

Continue knitting Argyle pattern rnds 5–10 and then rep rows 1–10 until total work measures 9¾ in/24.8 cm. This length can also be adjusted to suit individual hand size.

TOP OF MITTEN

Rnds 1–8: Knit in A.

Bind off using the gather method (see page 112).

Finishing

With right side facing out, pull gently on the yarn gathering just the edges of the top of each mitten (to round), and then seam the top closed using mattress stitch. Fold thumb in half lengthwise with right sides facing out, and seam sides of thumb closed using mattress stitch. Weave in ends.

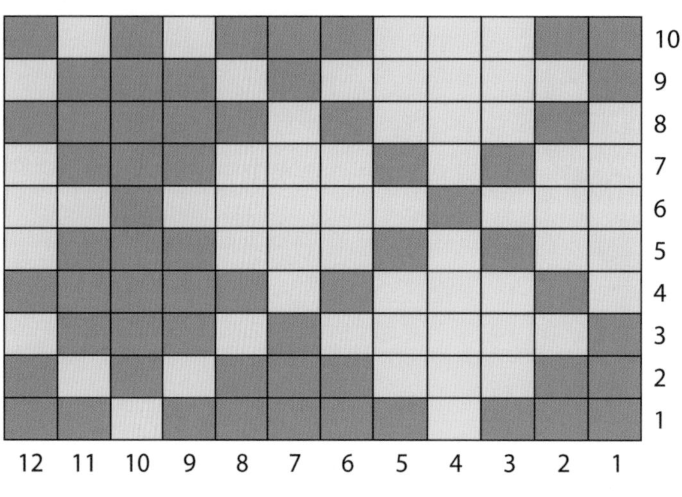

Marble Heather (A)

Cornmeal (B)

Polygon
Shawl

This lovely shawl is decreased on one side only, forming a right triangle. Combining mesh lace and garter sections with hand-dyed yarn adds interest and substance to this modern wrap.

Level

Intermediate

Finished Measurements

21 in/53.3 cm at widest point x 60 in/152.4 cm long

Gauge

16 sts and 32 rows = 4 in/10.2 cm in garter stitch

Yarn

Miss Babs Madison, Aran weight #4 (100% superwash merino wool; 200 yd/182.8 m, 5.8 oz/160 g per skein)
1 skein Blue Slate (MC)
1 skein Biker Chick—Babette (CC)

Supplies

- ⅜ in/1 cm peg spacing loom with 80 pegs
- Knitting tool
- Crochet hook
- Measuring tape
- ***Optional:*** Blocking wires are recommended if you would like perfectly straight sides. You may also find stitch markers helpful.

Pattern Notes

- A wool or natural fiber is recommended to best show off the mesh work and for blocking purposes.
- Hand-dyed yarn is rarely duplicated, and colorways come and go quickly; choose two complementary colors for your project, and it will be as unique as your handwork.
- The shawl is knit flat and decreased on one side only.

Pattern

Foundation row: Chain CO 80 pegs with 1 strand MC; work as flat panel.
Row 1: Skip1, knit to end of row.
Row 2: Skip1, purl to last stitch, k1.
Row 3: As row 1.

RIDGED MESH LACE PATTERN

Row 1: Skip1, k4, *ssk-yo; rep from * to last 5 sts, k3, k2tog (some rows will have an extra stitch, k4, k2tog on those rows).
Row 2: Skip1, p4, knit to last 4 sts, p3, k1.
Row 3: Skip1, k4, *yo, k2tog; rep from * to last 4 sts, k4 (on rows with 5 sts at the end, k5).
Row 4: Skip1, p4, knit to last 4 sts, p3, k1.
Rows 5–12: Rep rows 1–4 (2 times).
Stop knitting with MC; change to CC.
Row 13: Skip1, knit to end of row.
Row 14: Skip1, purl to last st, k1.
Rows 15–16: Rep rows 13 and 14 (1 time).
Rep rows 1–16 (2 times).
Rep rows 1–12 (1 time).

GARTER SECTION

Row 1: Skip1, knit to last 2 sts, k2tog.
Row 2: Skip1, purl to last st, k1.
Row 3: Skip1, knit to end of row.
Row 4: Skip1, purl to last st, k1.
Rows 5–40: Rep rows 1–4 (9 times).

Rep Ridged Mesh Lace and Garter Section until there is only 1 stitch left on the loom; bind off. The last 2 sections are done as the Garter Section, beginning when you have approximately 16 stitches remaining on the loom.

Finishing

Weave in ends and block wrap on wires for best results and straightest edges.

Blue Bayou Cowl

Two-color brioche makes a stretchy, reversible, lofty fabric that has unlimited potential just by changing yarn colors. Make it subtle (as in the sample cowl) or dramatic, using contrasting colors such as black and white. As a bonus, it's also fast and easy to do on the loom!

Level

Confident Beginner

Finished Measurements

8 in/20.3 cm high x 22 in/55.9 cm circumference

Gauge

16 sts and 26 rows = 4 in/10.2 cm square in brioche stitch

Yarn

Cozy Color Works Worsted Weight Merino, worsted weight #4 (100% superwash merino; 200 yd/182.8 m, 3.5–4.5 oz/ 99–127.5 g per skein)
1 Skein Blue Steel (A)
1 Skein Bayou (B)

Supplies

- ⅜ in/1 cm peg spacing loom using 88 pegs
- Knitting tool
- Crochet hook
- Measuring tape

Special Stitches

brk (brioche knit): Use the regular knit st, but you will knit 2 sts together as one.
brp (brioche purl): Use the regular purl st, but you will purl 2 sts together as one.

Pattern Notes

- Cowl is knit in the round.
- Gauge is not crucial to this pattern; you may use the regular knit stitch or u-knit where knit is indicated.
- It takes 2 rounds to complete one row of brioche stitch; they will be indicated as rnds 1a and 1b.
- Brk/brp are worked as regular knit/purl sts, but you will work 2 sts together on those pegs.
- This is a loom-friendly pattern and can be easily adapted to any round loom (cowl size) with even peg numbers; just adjust your yarn weight to coordinate with your loom gauge.

Pattern

Foundation round: Chain CO 88 pegs with 1 strand of Color A; join to work in the round.
Rnd 1: Knit.
Rnd 2: Purl.
Rnd 3: Knit.

BRIOCHE STITCH (MULTIPLE OF 2 STS)

Set-up round (Color A): *Skip1 wyif, k1, rep from * to end of round.
Set-up round (Color B): *Brp1, skip1 wyif, rep from * to end of round.
Rnd 1a (Color A): *Skip1 wyif, brk1, rep from * to end of round.
Rnd 1b (Color B): *Brp1, skip1 wyif, rep from * to end of round.
Rep rnds 1a and 1b until work measures 8 in/20.3 cm.

TOP BORDER

Cut Color B and knit in Color A only.
Rnd 1: Knit.
Rnd 2: Purl.
Rnd 3: Knit.
Chain one bind-off.

Finishing

Weave in ends. Blocking is optional.

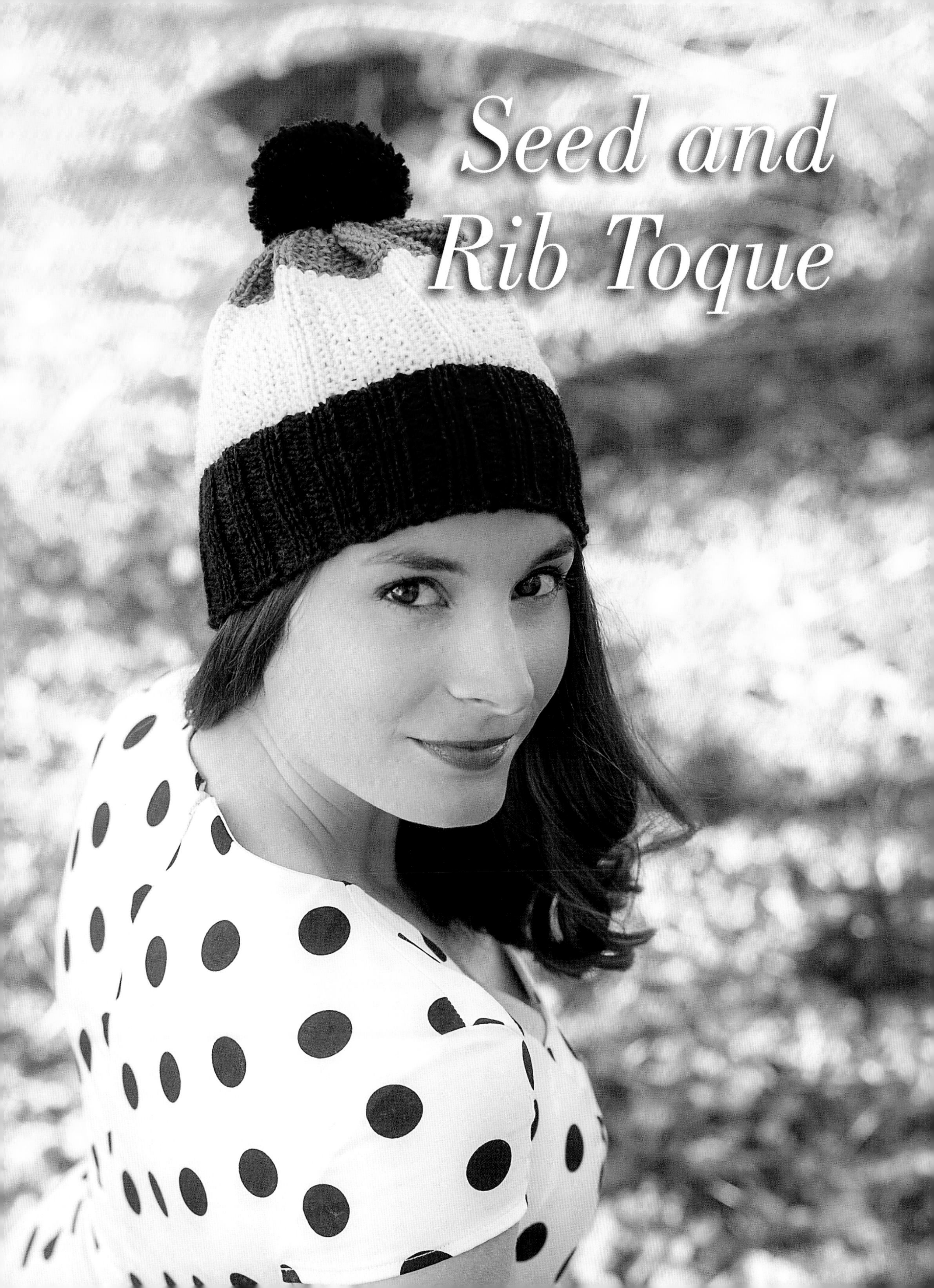
Seed and
Rib Toque

A combination of ribbing and interrupted seed stitch creates a comfortable beanie that is both warm and stylish. Dress this hat up or down. Easy enough for a beginner!

Level

Beginner

Finished Measurements

8½ in/21.6 cm high x 20 in/50.8 cm circumference, to fit adult/teen

Gauge

18 sts and 30 rows = 4 in/10.2 cm in 2x2 rib stitch

16 sts and 40 rows = 4 in/10.2 cm in interrupted seed stitch

Yarn

Cascade Yarns Cascade 220, worsted weight #4 (100% Peruvian Highland Wool; 220 yd/200 m, 3.5 oz/100 g per skein)

1 skein #8393 Navy (MC)

1 skein #8010 Natural (CC)

1 skein #2415 Sunflower (CC1)

Supplies

- ⅜ in/1 cm peg spacing round loom with 80 pegs
- Knitting tool
- Crochet hook
- 3 in/7.6 cm pom-pom maker

Pattern Notes

- Hat is knit in the round, starting at the bottom.
- Hat is worked in multiples of 10 sts.
- For photo-illustrated instructions on how to work the u-knit stitch, see page 114.

Pattern

Foundation round: Chain CO all pegs with 1 strand MC; join to work in the round.
Rnd 1: *U-k2, p2, rep from * to end of round.
Rep rnd 1 until total work measures 3 in/7.6 cm. Cut MC and begin knitting with CC.

PATTERN STITCH

Rnd 1: U-k.
Rnd 2: *U-k2, [u-k1, p1] 4 times, rep from * to end of round.
Rnd 3: *U-k2, [p1, u-k1] 4 times, rep from * to end of round.
Rep rnds 2 and 3 until total work measures 6 in/15.25 cm. Cut CC and begin knitting with CC1.
Rep rnds 1–3 and then rep rnds 2 and 3 until total knitting measures 8½ in/21.6 cm for fitted hat or 9½ in/24.1 cm for slouchy hat.
Bind off all sts using the gather method.

Finishing

Weave in ends and make a 3 in/7.6 cm pom-pom for top of hat (optional). Blocking of hat is optional.

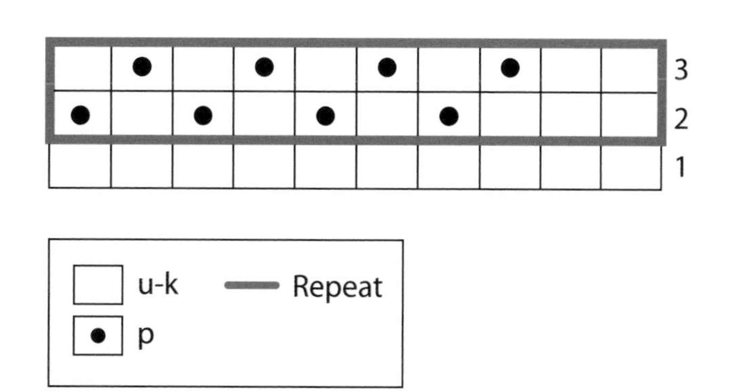

Autumn Welted Toque

Plenty of texture and a thick weave create a hat that is sure to keep your head warm during cold winters. The "welts" are formed by ridges made from alternating knit and purl sections. Simple stitches will make easy work of this pretty toque!

Level

Beginner

Finished Measurements

8½ in/21.6 cm high x 22 in/55.9 circumference

Gauge

16 sts and 46 rows = 4 in/10.2 cm square in welted garter stitch

Yarn

Lion Brand Landscapes, worsted weight #4 (100% acrylic; 147 yd/134 m, 3.5 oz/100 g per skein)
2 skeins #204 Desert Spring

Supplies

- ⅜ in/1 cm peg spacing round loom with 80 pegs
- Knitting tool
- Measuring tape
- Crochet hook
- 1 in/2.5 cm pom-pom maker or cardboard (optional)

Pattern Notes

- Hat is knit in the round from the bottom and then gathered at the top.
- Brim is designed to roll at the edge.
- This is a loom-friendly pattern and can be worked on virtually any loom. Just match your yarn to the loom gauge and work to the desired length.

Pattern

Foundation round: Chain CO all 80 pegs; join to work in the round.

Rnds 1–7: Knit.

Rnds 8–10: Purl.

Rnds 11–13: Knit.

Rep rnds 8–13 alternating knit and purl sections until total work measures 8½ in/21.6 cm. End work on a knit section to reduce bulk when gathering hat.

Bind off using gather method (see page 112).

Finishing

Weave in ends. Add 1 in/2.5 cm pom-pom to top of hat (optional).

On-a-Roll Mitts

An everyday, sporty-style mitt, this is an easy loom knit, perfect for those evenings when you want to relax with a quick project. Try it in your favorite team colors for different looks.

Level

Beginner

Sizes/Finished Measurements

Ladies Small/Medium (Large). Instructions are written for size Small/Medium, with instructions for size Large in parentheses. If only one instruction is given, it applies to both sizes.

Length: 13½ (13½) in/34.3 (34.3) cm

Circumference: 9 (10) in/22.9 (25.5) cm

Gauge

17 sts and 26 rows = 4 in/10.2 cm square in stockinette stitch

Yarn

Patons Classic Wool Worsted, worsted weight #4 (100% wool; 210 yd/192 m, 3.5 oz/100 g per skein)

1 skein #00224 Grey Mix (MC)

1 skein #00201 Winter White (CC)

Supplies

- ⅜ in/1 cm peg spacing round or adjustable loom with 36 (small/medium) or 40 (large) pegs
- Knitting tool
- Crochet hook
- Yarn/tapestry needle

Pattern Notes

- Mitt is worked in the round until the thumb. Thumb is then worked flat, and the mitt is finished by working in the round again.
- Top of mitt is designed to roll.

Pattern (make 2)

Foundation row: Chain CO 36 (40) pegs with 1 strand MC; join to work in the round.
Rnd 1: *K2, p1, rep from * to last st, k1.
Rnd 2: K1, *p1, k2, rep from * to last 2 sts, p1, k1.
Rnd 3–8: Rep rnds 1 and 2 (3 times).
Cut MC and change to CC.
Rnd 9: Knit.
Rnds 10–17: Rep rnds 1–8.
Cut CC and change to MC.
Rnd 18: Knit.
Rep rnd 18 until knitting measures 8½ in/21.6 cm.

THUMB

Stop knitting in the round and knit over 7 pegs only.
Rows 1–14: Knit.
Rows 15–17: *K1, p1, rep from * to last st, k1.
Bind off 7 sts.

Second Side of Thumb

Chain CO 7 pegs (the same pegs that you worked the first side of the thumb on).
Rows 1–3: *K1, p1, rep from * to last st, k1.
Rows 4–17: Knit.

TOP OF MITT

Begin knitting in the round again.
Rnds 1–4: Knit.
Change to CC.
Rnds 5–12: Knit in CC.
Change to MC.
Rnd 13: Knit.
Rep rnd 13 until mitt measures 13½ in/34.3 cm or desired length.

Finishing

Weave in ends. Seam both sides of thumb closed with mattress stitch.

LOOM KNITTING STITCHES AND TECHNIQUES

Casting On the Loom

CHAIN CAST-ON (CHAIN CO)

1. Place a slipknot on the holding peg or on peg 1 if no holding peg is available.

2. Place loom so that you are working from inside the loom.

3. Place working yarn between the first and last peg and wrap around crochet hook, then take working yarn to front of peg. Now grab the working yarn with the crochet hook and pull it between pegs 1 and 2 and through the loop on the hook.

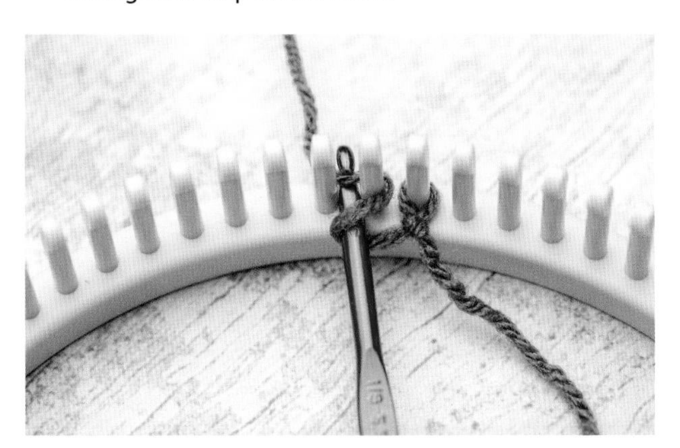

4. Continue in this manner until the required number of sts/pegs are cast-on.

To join to work in the round: If you are working in the round, put your last loop on peg 1; there will be 2 loops on this peg now. They will be knit as one on the next row. (This does not apply to flat panel knitting.)

TRUE CABLE CAST-ON (CO1)

This cast-on is often used to increase in the middle of a project. When directed to CO1, use this method.

1. Place slipknot on peg 1.

2. Go between pegs 1 and 2 with working yarn and lay yarn above loop created by slipknot.

3. Reach up through slipknot and grab working yarn (as in regular knit stitch), creating a new loop.

4. Flip this loop (top of loop should now face downward) and place it on peg 2.

5. Take working yarn behind peg 2 (before placing the new loop on the peg) and repeat until all pegs are cast-on.

KITCHENER CAST-ON (USED FOR SOCK KNITTING)

1. Secure the yarn on the holding peg; then take it around the 1st peg on your loom and around the last peg on your loom.

2. Next, take it around peg 2, then the second to the last peg and so on, always going to the outside of each peg. Continue in this way until all pegs on the loom are wrapped. Allow the working yarn to hang next to the last peg.

3. Using the regular knit stitch, lock in your wraps by knitting one row. The photo shows what your loom will look like after all wraps are knit.

4. Continue as your pattern states, working the toe and foot.

5. Once your sock is long enough, and beginning on the side opposite the holding peg, tighten each loop one by one. Pull gently until all loops are tightened.

6. The cast-on will be almost invisible, with no seam.

Binding Off the Loom

GATHER METHOD

1. After finishing your last row, wrap your working yarn 2 times around your loom and cut.

2. Thread end of yarn through yarn/tapestry needle.

3. Take needle down through 1st peg; repeat for all remaining pegs.

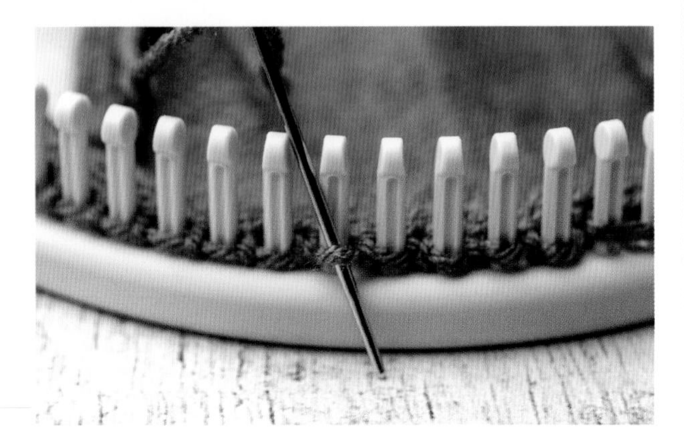

4. Pull the stitches off the loom and gently pull on the yarn tail to gather knitting, and secure by weaving in end.

CHAIN ONE BIND-OFF AND CHAIN TWO BIND-OFF

1. Place loop on peg 1 onto crochet hook.

2. Grab working yarn and pull through loop (creating a chain one). If you are working the chain one bind-off stop here. If you are working the chain two bind-off, repeat this step (creating a chain 2).

3. Place loop from peg 2 onto crochet hook and pull through the loop already on the crochet hook.

4. Repeat steps 2 and 3 until all loops on pegs are removed. If working the chain two bind-off, only chain one on the last stitch.

5. Weave in yarn end.

EXTRA-STRETCHY BIND-OFF (X-STRETCHY BO, WORKING IN THE ROUND)

1. Wrap your working yarn 3 times around your loom and cut.

2. Thread end of working yarn through a tapestry needle.

3. Insert the needle down through the stitch on the first peg. Do not remove your sts from the loom until step 7.

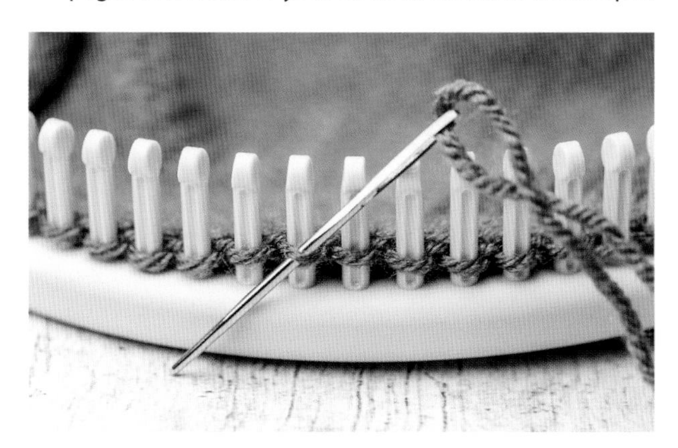

4. Insert the needle up through the stitch on the previous peg.

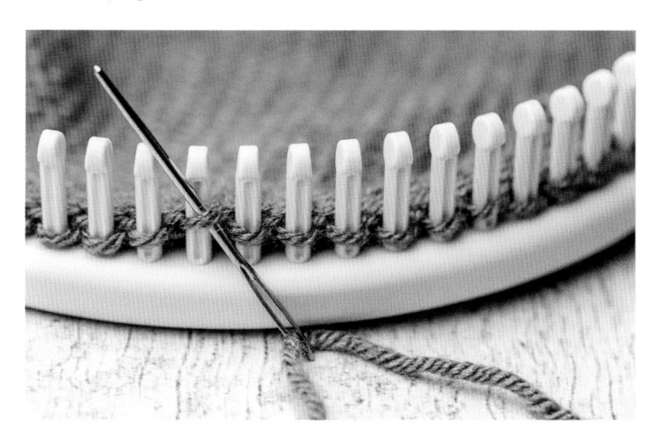

5. Take your working yarn behind the first/adjacent peg and go to the next peg. Take your needle down through the stitch on the second/next peg.

6. Repeat steps 4–5 all the way around the loom, finishing on peg 1.

7. Remove the stitches from the pegs and weave in end.

Stitches

REGULAR KNIT STITCH (K)

This stitch has similar tension to the knit stitch used in needle knitting.

1. Lay the working yarn above the existing stitch on the peg.

2. Insert knitting tool upward through loop and grab working yarn.

3. Pull working yarn down through loop, creating a new loop.

4. Pull with the pick or your fingers so that the existing loop comes off the peg.

5. Place the new stitch on the peg. The regular knit stitch is now complete.

U-KNIT STITCH (U-K)

This is an easy knit stitch to learn and produces a medium-tension stitch.

1. Push existing loops down to the bottom of loom.

2. Lay working yarn above existing loop but place between the peg you are knitting and the next peg.

3. Pull bottom loop over working yarn. The u-knit stitch is now complete.

E-WRAP KNIT (EWK)

Also known as the twisted stockinette stitch, this produces the loosest weave of all the knit stitches. It does not produce the traditional "V" of regular stockinette stitch.

1. Working back to front, wind the working yarn around the peg once.

2. Pull the bottom loop over the top loop.

PURL STITCH (P)

1. Push the already existing loop to the top of peg.

2. Place working yarn under the existing loop on peg.

3. Reach down through top loop and grab working yarn, forming a new loop.

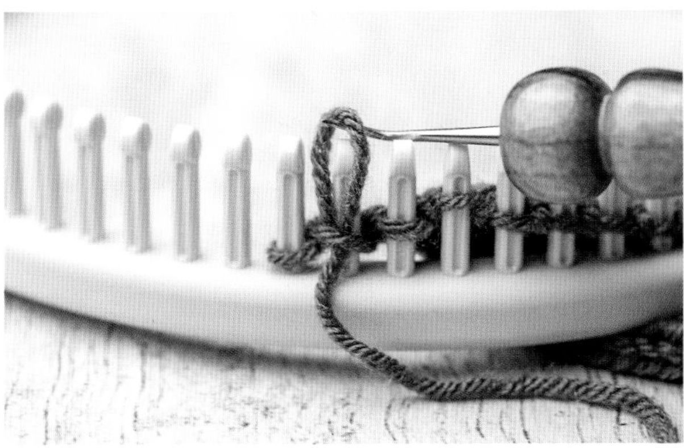

4. Pull the stitch off the peg using your fingers or the pick, keeping hold of the newly formed loop.

5. Place the newly formed stitch onto the peg.

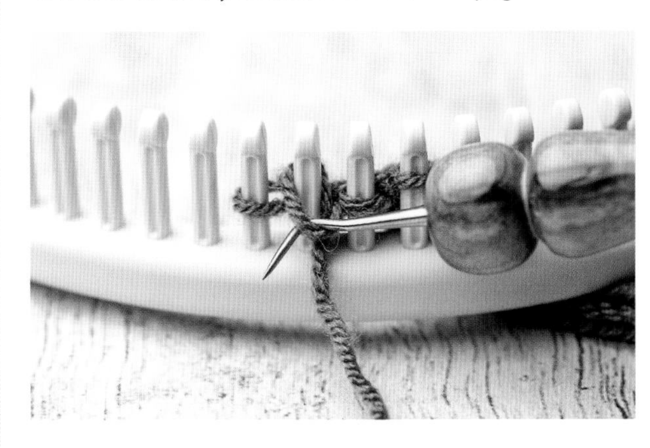

SKIP 1 (SKIP1) WITH YARN IN BACK (WYIB) OR WITH YARN IN FRONT (WYIF)

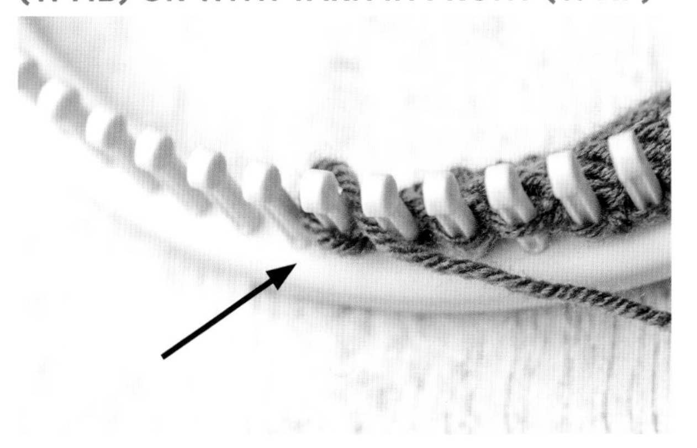

The indicated peg has been skipped by taking the working yarn behind it without working the stitch and preparing to work the next peg. If wyif is indicated, place the working yarn in front of the peg without working the stitch.

RIGHT TWIST (RTW, WORKED OVER 2 PEGS)

1. Place the stitch from peg 2 on a stitch holder.

2. Pick up the stitch on peg 1 with your knitting tool and put it on peg 2.

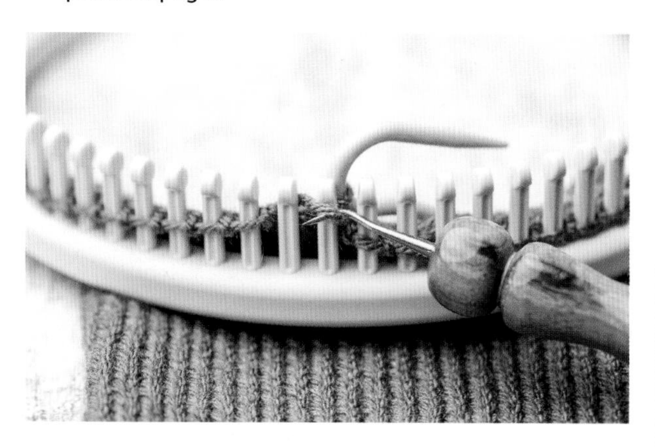

3. Transfer the stitch on the holder to peg 1 and remove the holder.

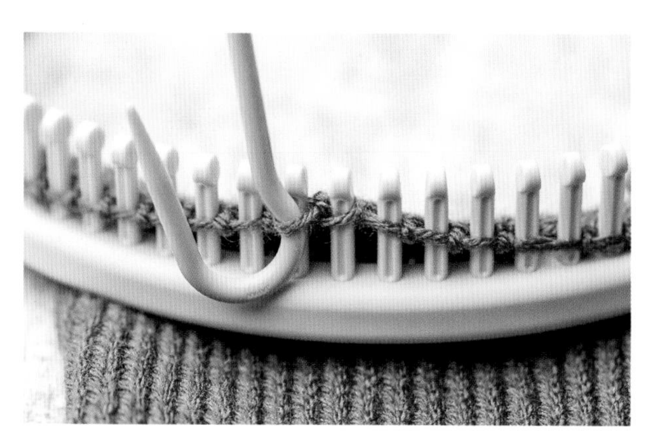

4. Knit pegs 1 and 2 using the knit stitch indicated in the pattern. Right twist completed.

LEFT TWIST (LTW, WORKED OVER 2 PEGS)

1. Place the stitch from peg 1 on a stitch holder.

2. Pick up the stitch on peg 2 with your knitting tool and put it on peg 1.

3. Transfer the stitch on the holder to peg 2 and remove the holder.

4. Knit pegs 1 and 2 using the knit stitch indicated in the pattern. Left twist completed.

4-STITCH RIGHT CROSS CABLE (4-ST RC)

1. Place the stitches from pegs 1 and 2 onto cable needles and position them to the inside of the loom, behind the pegs.

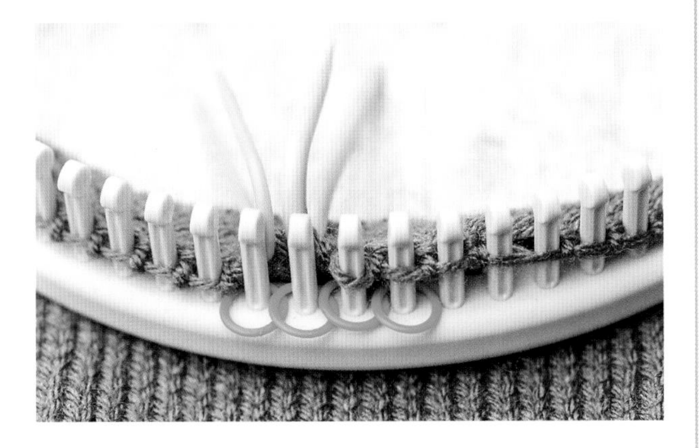

2. Knit peg 3; then, with the knitting tool, move the stitch to peg 1, being careful not to twist it. Knit peg 4, then move it to peg 2. In the photo, the stitches have been knit and moved.

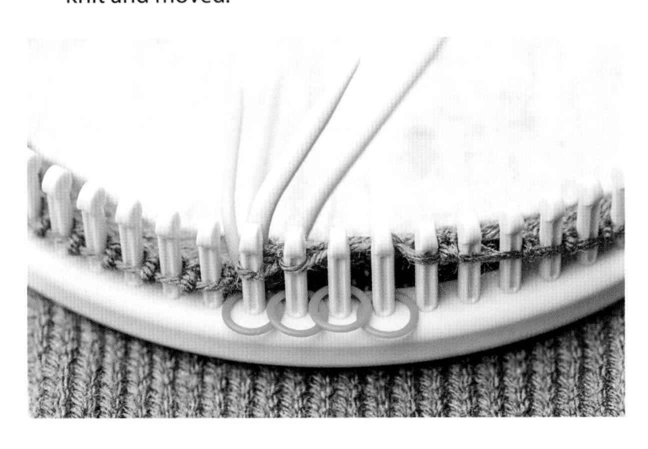

3. Transfer the stitch from peg 1 being held on the green cable needle to peg 3, and transfer the stitch from peg 2 being held on the pink cable needle to peg 4.

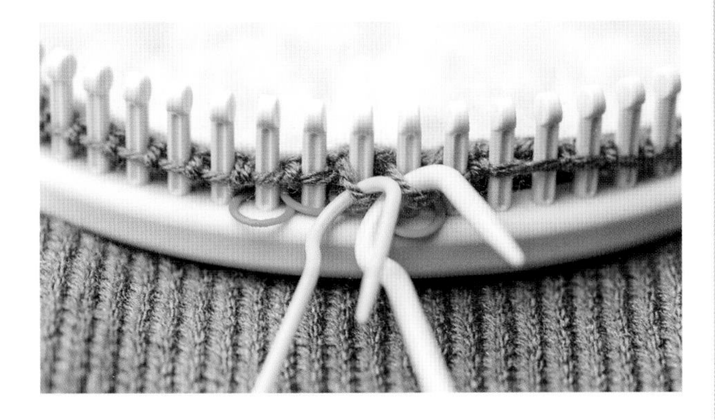

4. Knit pegs 3 and 4.

5. Pull gently on all stitches to tighten and even them out.

WRAP AND TURN (W&T, WORKED OVER 1 PEG)

1. Knit/purl to where the w&t is called for; take the stitch off the next peg and hold it with your knitting tool.

2. Wrap around the back of the now empty peg by coming behind and to the front of the peg. Place the stitch from your knitting tool back on the peg.

3. With working yarn, knit or purl back in the opposite direction without knitting the peg you did the W&T on.

Note: The wrap and turn can also be done by eliminating step 1 and placing the wrap above the already existing loop; this is best done on the edges of a garment and not within the knitting, as with socks and similar items.

YARN OVER (YO)

A yarn over can be completed two ways in loom knitting: by e-wrapping the peg (less tension; see below) or by laying the yarn on top of the peg and moving on to the next stitch (more tension, exactly as a skip1 wyif). If it's not indicated in the pattern, you may use whichever method is most comfortable for you. If an e-wrap (ew) is indicated, always e-wrap. The e-wrap method is also recommended for tight knitters who have difficulty moving their stitches.

E-WRAP PEG (WRAP PEG)

To e-wrap a peg, wind your working yarn completely around the peg, from back to front. If you are working counterclockwise around the loom, you will wrap the peg in a clockwise direction. If you are working clockwise, you will wrap the peg in a counterclockwise direction. Do not knit as you would when an e-wrap knit (ewk) is asked for.

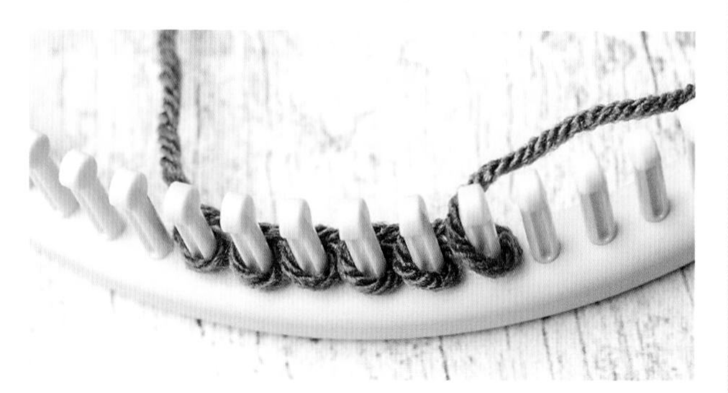

Here is a series of pegs wrapped in a clockwise direction. The pegs are wrapped from back to front. The knitter is working counterclockwise.

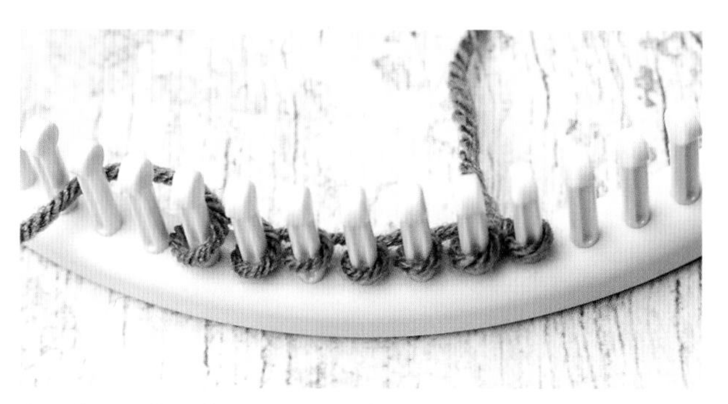

Here is a series of pegs wrapped in a counterclockwise direction. The pegs are wrapped from back to front. The knitter is working clockwise.

SHIFT 3, YARN OVER (SH3-YO)

Shift 3 stitches toward the outside edge and then yarn over. Takes place over the first 4 pegs at the beginning of a row.

1. Take the stitch from peg 2 and put it on peg 1.

2. Take the stitch from peg 3 and put it on peg 2.

3. Take the stitch from peg 4 and put it on peg 3.

4. K2tog on peg 1, knit pegs 2 and 3.

5. E-wrap peg 4, completing the yarn over; do not knit.

YARN OVER, SHIFT 3 (YO-SH3)

Yarn over and then shift 3 stitches toward the outside edge. Takes place over the last 4 stitches of a row.

1. Take the stitch from peg 3 and put it on peg 4, the outside peg.

2. Take the stitch from peg 2 and put it on peg 3.

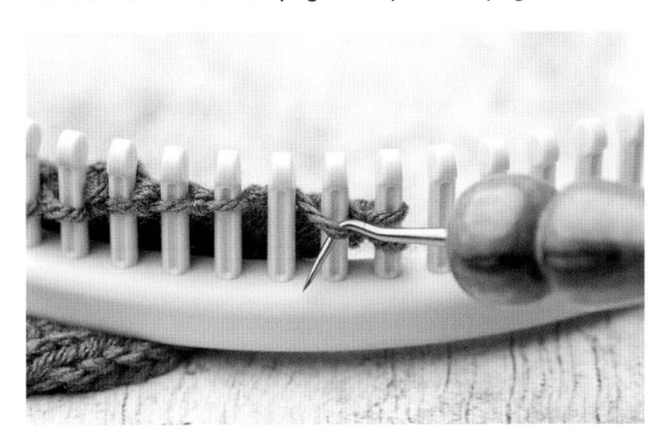

3. Take the stitch from peg 1 and put it on peg 2.

4. E-wrap peg 1 to complete the yarn over; do not knit.

5. Knit pegs 2 and 3, k2tog on peg 4.

MAKE BOBBLE (MB, TAKES PLACE OVER 1 PEG)

1. Make an e-wrap knit stitch by making the e-wrap and lifting the bottom loop over the top wrap. You may place the first e-wrap knit stitch on a cable needle for easier lifting later (optional).

2. Make 4 more e-wrap knit stitches on the same peg, for a total of 5.

3. Reach down below peg and pick up first e-wrap knit stitch made and lift it onto the peg. Optionally, use the cable needle to lift the first stitch up onto the peg.

4. E-wrap knit all stitches on peg together as one.

KNIT 2 TOGETHER (K2TOG) OR PURL 2 TOGETHER (P2TOG)

1. Move the stitch from peg 1 to peg 2.

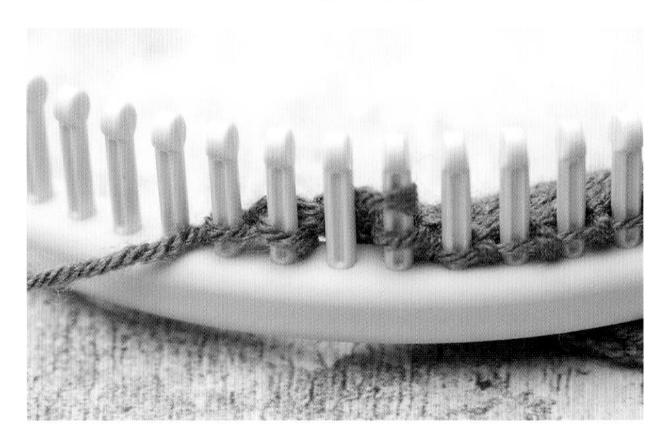

2. Move all outer stitches inward to fill the empty peg that was made; be sure to keep the stitches in their original order.

3. Knit/purl both loops/stitches on peg 2 as one over working yarn. One stitch decreased.

E-WRAP K2TOG/P2TOG (ALSO KNOWN AS THE YO-K2TOG/P2TOG)

1. Lift stitch from peg 1 and place it on peg 2.

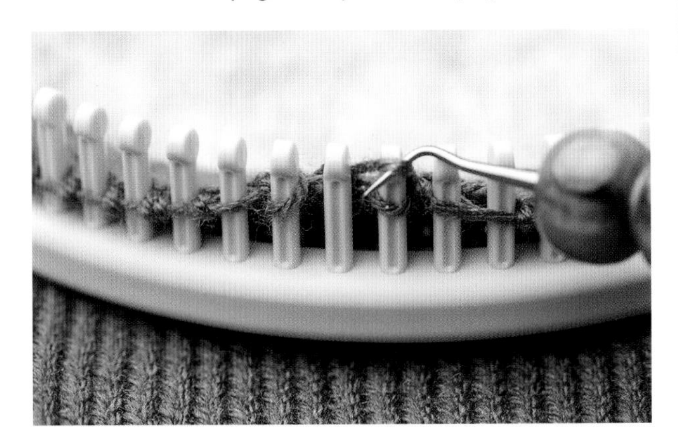

2. E-wrap peg 1 to create a yarn over. You may also lay the yarn across the peg as in a skip1 wyif when the pattern does not require the e-wrap (ew).

3. Knit/purl both stitches on peg 2 as one.

4. On the next row, knit the yarn over on peg 1 as you would any other stitch.

SLIP, SLIP, KNIT (SSK)

1. Move the stitch from peg 2 to peg 1.

2. Move all outer stitches inward to fill the empty peg that was made; be sure to keep the stitches in their original order.

3. Knit both stitches on peg 1 together as one. One stitch decreased.

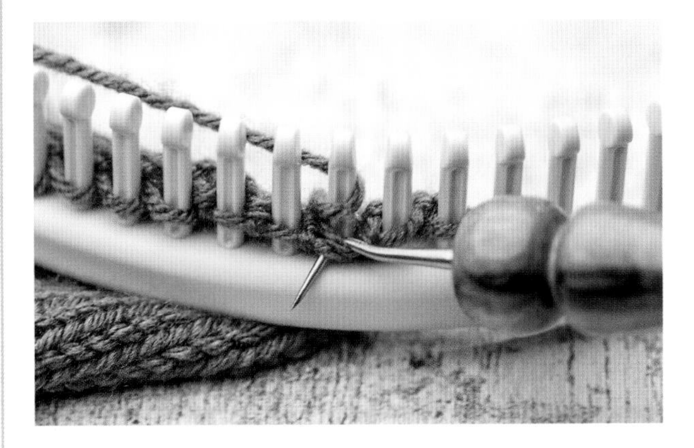

SLIP, SLIP, KNIT, E-WRAP YARN AROUND EMPTY PEG (SSK-EW) (ALSO KNOWN AS THE SSK-YO)

1. Move the stitch from peg 2 to peg 1.

2. Knit the stitches on peg 1 together as one.

3. Wrap the empty peg and bring the working yarn to the outside of the next peg.

PASS THE SLIPPED STITCH OVER (PSSO, WORKED OVER 3 PEGS)

1. Move the stitch from peg 1 to peg 2.

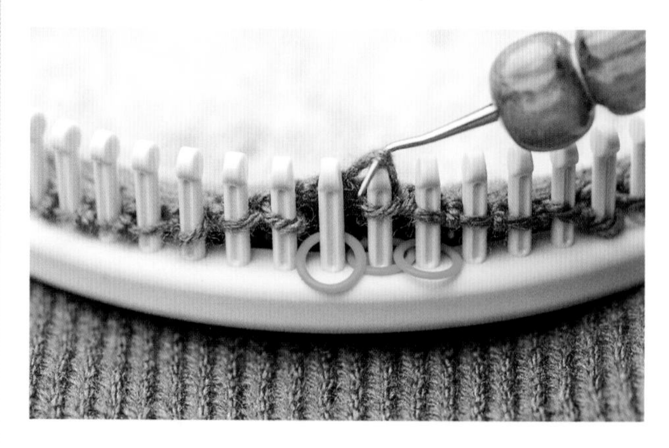

2. Move the stitch from peg 3 to peg 2.

3. E-wrap peg 1 and prepare to work the stitches on peg 2.

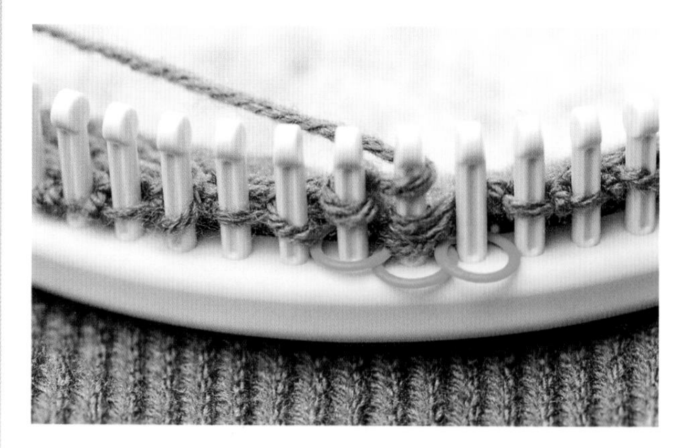

4. Knit all sts together on peg 2.

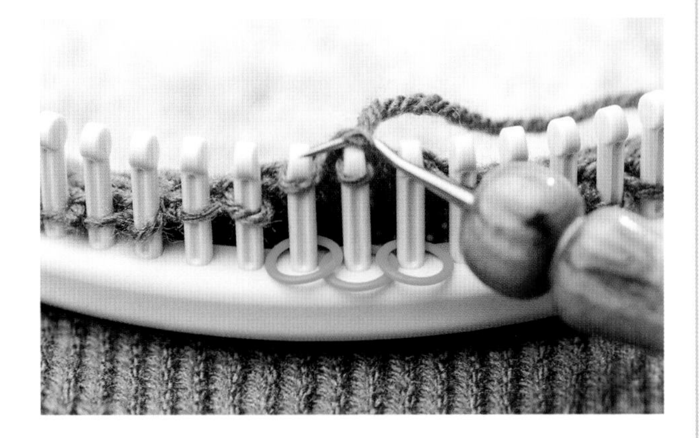

5. E-wrap peg 3.

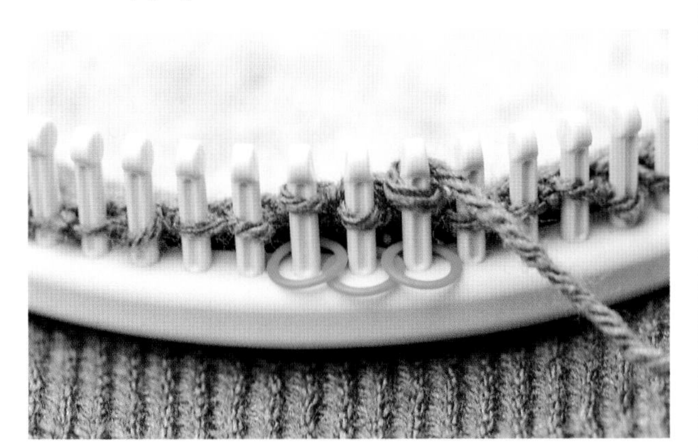

Moving Stitches for Lace Knitting

COUNT FORWARD (CF)

Count forward the indicated number of pegs. Always begin counting from the next peg to be worked.

Always begin counting from the next peg to be worked. To help you keep track, pull the working yarn forward between the last and next peg to be worked.

A count forward will always have a number next to it. In this example, the knitter has counted forward 3 pegs and moved that stitch forward 1, performing a cf3-mf1.

MOVE BACK (MB)

Pick up the stitch and move the stitch back the indicated number of pegs.

In this example, the knitter has counted forward 3 pegs and moved that stitch back 1, completing a cf3-mb1.

In this example, the knitter has counted forward 4 pegs and moved that stitch back 1 peg, completing a cf4-mb1.

MOVE FORWARD (MF)

Pick the stitch up and move it forward the indicated number of pegs.

In this example, the knitter has counted forward 4 pegs and moved that stitch forward 1 peg, completing a cf4-mf1.

FILL GAP (FG)

When many stitches must be moved, you'll see "fg" within your pattern. Move all stitches forward to fill the gap made by the stitch movement, and make room for the yarn over.

1. In this example, you see 2 stitches on the peg to the right, and the adjacent stitch is being moved forward onto the first empty peg.

2. The next stitch is moved forward.

3. The last and final stitch is being moved forward, filling the gap made by the initial stitch movement and making room for the yarn over on the peg next to the working yarn.

Special Skills

MAKING A HAT BRIM AND LIFTING STITCHES ONTO THE LOOM

In loom knitting you will often be asked to lift your stitches for hat brims and stitches like the puff stitch.

1. If making a hat brim, you will reach down to the first row of stitches and grab the stitch that is in line with the peg you are working on. For a hat brim, it is easiest to work from peg 1 to the last peg. Here you see the knitter has grabbed a stitch from the cast-on row and is placing it on the peg above and in line with the proper stitch column.

2. Place that stitch onto the loom.

3. Treat the 2 loops that are now on your loom as if they are one when you knit or purl the next row, unless otherwise indicated within your pattern.

WEAVING IN ENDS

You always want to leave a 4 to 5 in/10 to 13 cm tail of yarn at the end of your knitting. To keep this tail from being unsightly, you must weave it into the back of your knitting to hide it. You can do this with either a crochet hook or a yarn needle.

If using a crochet hook, insert it through the backs of stitches and then grab the tail and pull it through the knitting to hide.

If using a yarn needle, thread it with the tail and pull it through the bumps on the back of your knitting, going in and out, until the tail is completely hidden.

FAIR ISLE/STRANDED KNITTING

Stranded, or Fair Isle, knitting is a technique that uses two colors in the same row, allowing the knitter to create different patterns and motifs. Fair Isle knitting can be done with two different methods.

Method 1: Using the main color, knit all stitches that call for that color, ignoring all other stitches. Keep working yarn behind pegs that are not to be knit. Drop main color (A); then pick up coordinating color (B) and knit stitches that require that color. This method keeps your colors untwisted.

Method 2: In this method, you carry both the main color (A) and coordinating color (B) down the row together. When the pattern calls for the A, place the B on top of the A and drop the B; then knit with the A, and reverse this when using the B to knit. This effectively twists the A and B together as you work down the row.

When working stranded knitting as in method 2, place the nonworking yarn on top of the working yarn and drop it as you knit with the working yarn.

The working yarn has been pulled to the front and is ready to work the next peg, locking in the nonworking yarn.

PICKING UP EDGE STITCHES

1. Place project inside loom with the right side facing you.

2. Using the knitting tool, loosen the first stitch along the edge of fabric and place it on the loom. Be careful not to twist the stitch as you are lifting it, and be careful to pick up only one stitch.

3. Continue in this manner until the indicated number of stitches are lifted (refer to your pattern).

3-STITCH I-CORD

This I-cord is worked over 3 pegs using the knit stitch (use whichever knit stitch is used in the pattern you are working).

1. Chain or e-wrap cast on 3 pegs, if needed.

2. Knit peg 1.

3. Go behind peg 2; knit peg 3.

4. Knit peg 2.

5. Repeat above sequence, pulling gently downward on knitting, until desired length is reached, and bind off.

If you would like to taper the end of your I-cord:

1. Move peg 1 to peg 2, knit both loops over working yarn (k2tog).

2. Move peg 3 to peg 2, knit both loops over working yarn (ssk).

3. Bind off.

SINGLE CROCHET EDGING

1. Insert a crochet hook through the first row of stitches, front to back, and place the working yarn over the top of the hook (yarn over).

2. Pull the hook and yarn back up through the knitting to the front.

3. Insert the hook into the next stitch to your left/right. Wrap the working yarn over the hook, and pull through the two loops on your crochet hook.

4. Continuing to insert the hook through the next stitch, repeat steps 1–3.

MATTRESS STITCH/SEAM

The mattress stitch creates an invisible vertical seam. Use the same yarn or a similar color as in your project (here I used a contrasting color for illustration purposes only).

1. Lay your two pieces side by side, with right sides facing up.

2. Stretch your knitting a little and find the first row of ladder stitches near the edge of each panel.

3. Using a yarn needle, go under the first ladder stitch on one panel (back to front).

4. Now go to the opposite panel and go under the first ladder stitch on that piece (again, back to front).

5. Repeat, alternating sides, until you are at the end of the piece to be seamed. Occasionally, pull gently on the working yarn, and your stitches will begin to blend together and look seamless. Do not pucker your knitting by pulling too hard.

6. Finish by connecting your top two corners together and weave in your end.

In this example, the yarn has been taken under the "ladder" stitches, first on one side and then the other. For demonstration purposes, I have used a bright-colored yarn, but you will use a color that matches your knitting. Also for demonstration purposes, I have shown the technique on the second row of ladders; you will do your stitching on the first row, closer to the edge.

The ends of the yarn have been pulled gently and you can no longer see the working yarn even though it is a bright color.

GARTER SEAM

1. Lay your two pieces side by side, right sides facing up.
2. Find the top and bottom loops of each stitch (they look like bumps) on the edge of each panel.
3. Using a yarn needle, go under the first bottom loop on one panel and the first top loop on the other panel.
4. Now, go back to the first panel and go under the next bottom loop.
5. Go under the next top loop on the other panel. This will allow the knitting to nestle neatly together.
6. Repeat, alternating panels, until you are at the top of your knitting.
7. Occasionally, pull gently on the knitting (not too hard; you don't want it to pucker), bringing it together.
8. Finish by connecting the top two corners together. Cut the yarn if necessary and weave in the end.

The working yarn has been taken first under the lower bump in the knitting on one side and then under the corresponding top bump on the other side. This will allow the garter stitch to nestle together once the seam is pulled snug. For demonstration purposes, the seam is being done one stitch over; you can seam closer to the edge.

The working yarn has been pulled gently and the stitches are now able to nestle together. When you use a matching yarn, your seam will be invisible.

ADDING A LIFELINE

A lifeline can be used while working lace or to mark a row. Its purpose is to save your work at different points for easier stitch removal when a mistake is made. I like to use elastic cord because it is slippery, easy to remove, and able to be reused over and over, but you may use scrap yarn also (this will take a little extra time to remove later). A lifeline can be a "life saver" when working intricate lace, as these stitches are difficult to walk backward. It can also be used to mark rows for lifting, such as with a hem. To insert a lifeline:

1. Thread a yarn/tapestry needle with elastic cord.

2. Take your needle down through every stitch/peg in use on your loom, leaving a 4 in/10.2 cm tail at either end (just like a gathered bind-off except you do not remove the stitches from the loom).

3. Leave the lifeline within your knitting and resume as the pattern states (it may be useful to write down the pattern row number in which you place the lifeline for future reference). If using elastic cord, the lifeline will easily slip out of the knitting when no longer needed.

4. If you make a mistake and need to use the lifeline, take your knitting off the loom and pull out the stitches back to the lifeline. Place each stitch saved on the lifeline back onto the loom pegs and continue knitting from that point.

QUICK STITCH GUIDE

k (knit) Lay the working yarn above the loop of the existing stitch on the peg. Insert knitting tool upward through loop and grab working yarn. Pull yarn down through loop, creating a new loop. Pull the original loop off the peg and place the new stitch on the peg.

k2tog (knit 2 together)
Move loop from peg 1 to peg 2, move loops from outer pegs inward to fill the gap made by the move, keeping stitches in their original order. Knit both stitches on peg 2 as one. In some patterns you will not need to move the stitches, as they have already been moved. This will be indicated in the pattern under special stitches.

p (purl) Push the existing loop to the top of the peg. Place working yarn under the loop on peg. Reach down through top loop and grab working yarn, forming a new loop. Pull the original stitch off the peg and place the newly formed stitch on the peg.

p2tog (purl 2 together)
Move loop from peg 1 to peg 2, move loops from outer pegs inward to fill the gap made by the move, keeping stitches in their original order. Purl both stitches on peg 2 as one.

psso (pass slipped stitch over)
Move the stitch from peg 1 to peg 2, and the stitch from peg 3 to peg 2. E-wrap peg 1. Knit all sts together on peg 2. E-wrap peg 3.

skip1 Skip the indicated peg by taking the working yarn behind it (wyib) or in front of it (wyif), as indicated.

ssk (slip, slip, knit)
Move the stitch from peg 2 to peg 1, and move all other stitches inward to fill the empty peg, keeping the stitches in order. Knit both stitches on peg 1.

ssk-yo/ssk-ew (slip, slip, knit, yarn over/e-wrap)
Move the stitch from peg 2 to peg 1, e-wrap the stitch on peg 2 or lay the working yarn on top of the peg as in a slip1 wyif. Always e-wrap the peg when you see ew indicated.

u-knit Push existing loops down to the bottom of the loom. Lay working yarn above existing loop but place between the peg you are knitting and the next peg. Pull bottom loop over working yarn.

w&t (wrap and turn)
Knit to where the w&t is called for; take the stitch off the next peg and hold it with your knitting tool. Wrap around the back of the now-empty peg and place the stitch from your knitting tool back on the peg. With working yarn, knit or purl back in the opposite direction without knitting the peg you did the w& t on.

yo/ew (yarn over or e-wrap)
When an e-wrap is called for, wrap the peg from front to back completely. If a yo is called for, you may e-wrap the peg or lay the working yarn on top of the peg as in a skip1 wyif (this will have more tension and is not recommended for lace or tight knitters).

yo-k2tog/p2tog; ew-k2tog/p2tog (yarn over/knit or purl 2 together; e-wrap/knit or purl 2 together)
Move the stitch from peg 1 to peg 2. E-wrap the empty peg. Knit or purl the stitches on peg 2 together as one. You may also lay the working yarn on top of peg 1 as in a skip1 wyif if the ew is not specifically indicated (not recommended for lace patterns or if you have difficulty moving your stitches).

ABBREVIATIONS

BO	bind-off
CC	coordinating color
cf	count forward
CO	cast-on
CO1	cast-on 1 st using the true cable cast-on method
ew-k2tog/p2tog	e-wrap/knit or purl 2 stitches together
ewk	e-wrap knit
fg	fill gap
k	regular knit stitch
k2tog	knit 2 stitches together
LTW	left twist
MB	make bobble
mb	move back
mf	move forward
MC	main color
p	purl stitch
p2tog	purl 2 stitches together
psso	pass the slipped stitch over
RTW	right twist
sh3-yo	shift 3 stitches, yarn over
ssk	slip, slip, knit
ssk-ew	slip, slip, knit, e-wrap peg
st(s)	stitch(es)
u-k	u-knit stitch
w&t	wrap and turn
wyib	with yarn in back of the peg
wyif	with yarn in front of the peg
yo	yarn over
yo-k2tog	yarn over, knit 2 together
yo-p2tog	yarn over, purl 2 together
yo-sh3	yarn over, shift 3 stitches

RESOURCES

Books

Cox, N. (2016), *Round Loom Knitting in 10 Easy Lessons*, Stackpole Books.

Mucklestone, M. J. (2011), *200 Fair Isle Motifs, A Knitter's Directory*, Interweave Books.

Myers, B., *Loom Lore,* http://loomlady.blogspot.com/, Kitchener Cast-on Method.

Rangel, A. (2017), *AlterKnit Stitch Dictionary, 200 Modern Knitting Motifs*, Interweave Books.

Shida, H. (2017), translated by Roehm, G., *Japanese Knitting Stitch Bible*, Tuttle Publishing.

Online Instruction

Further loom knitting instruction by Nicole F. Cox is available at the links below:

Video instruction, www.youtube.com/channel/UCmxMjlq7uUsTla2JxDtygxQ

Blog instruction, https://thismomentisgood.blogspot.com/

Looms

Boye
simplicity.com

CinDWood
cindwoodlooms.com

Cottage Looms
etsy.com/shop/cottagelooms

Knitting Board
knittingboard.com

Loops-n-Threads
michaels.com

Martha Stewart
lionbrand.com

Stitch Studio by Nicole
acmoore.com

ACKNOWLEDGMENTS

I'd like to thank the following people: My editor, Candi Derr, for her help, editing, and enthusiasm in bringing this idea, then book, to fruition. My publisher, editors, and art department for being unbelievably easy to work with and super talented; you are truly the best. My family, for their endless support and encouragement in all my creative endeavors. My models, for making my loom knitting designs look fabulous and being endlessly patient while I "get the shot." My husband, Ray Cox, for his help with the technical editing of the first draft of this book, "mad math skills," and photography/lighting assistance. My daughters, Amber and Danielle, for their assistance in styling, make-up, and "just being there" at any time, day or night, for whatever I needed. The loom knitting community, for which this book was written: you continue to amaze me with your ability to create and inspire.

VISUAL INDEX

Wilson

STITCH/TECHNIQUE INDEX